Eva Bischoff, Elisabeth Engel (Eds.)

Colonialism and Beyond

Periplus Studien

herausgegeben von

Andreas Eckert
Christoph Marx
Jürgen Zimmerer

Band 17

LIT

Colonialism and Beyond

Race and Migration from a Postcolonial Perspective

edited by

Eva Bischoff and Elisabeth Engel

LIT

Cover Picture:
Claus Zimmermann, *Our [e]motions [do not] bother them*, 2012
(Acryl hinter Glas, 44 × 30 cm).

The editors would like to thank the Gender Equality Office
of the John F. Kennedy Institute for North American Studies,
FU Berlin, for its financial support.

Bibliographic information published by the Deutsche Nationalbibliothek
The Deutsche Nationalbibliothek lists this publication in the Deutsche Nationalbibliografie; detailed bibliographic data are available in the Internet at http://dnb.d-nb.de.

ISBN 978-3-643-90261-0

A catalogue record for this book is available from the British Library

Klosbachstr. 107
CH-8032 Zürich
Tel. +41 (0) 44-251 75 05
Fax +41 (0) 44-251 75 06
E-Mail: zuerich@lit-verlag.ch
http://www.lit-verlag.ch

LIT VERLAG Dr. W. Hopf
Berlin 2013
Fresnostr. 2
D-48159 Münster
Tel. +49 (0) 2 51-620 320
Fax +49 (0) 2 51-23 19 72
E-Mail: lit@lit-verlag.de
http://www.lit-verlag.de

Distribution:
In Germany: LIT Verlag Fresnostr. 2, D-48159 Münster
Tel. +49 (0) 2 51-620 32 22, Fax +49 (0) 2 51-922 60 99, E-mail: vertrieb@lit-verlag.de

In Austria: Medienlogistik Pichler-ÖBZ, e-mail: mlo@medien-logistik.at
In Switzerland: B + M Buch- und Medienvertrieb, e-mail: order@buch-medien.ch
In the UK: Global Book Marketing, e-mail: mo@centralbooks.com
In North America: International Specialized Book Services, e-mail: orders@isbs.com

To Stefan Kleinwächter.

Table of Contents

Eva Bischoff and Elisabeth Engel 3
Colonialism and Beyond: Race and Migration from a Postcolonial Perspective

Olaf Stieglitz 20
Bodies in Motion: Writing Sport History as a History of Modern Bodies

Robert Júlio Decker 33
White Subjects, Governmentality, and Immigration Restriction in the United States, 1894-1924

Judith Schachter 53
Sovereignty, Identity, and Indigeneity: The Case of Hawai'i

Serhat Karakayali 72
Subject Citizen: The Ambiguity of Citizenship and its Colonial Laboratories

Manuela Bojadžijev 85
Connecting Some Dots: Migration, Colonialism, and Questions of Citizenship in Postcolonial Europe

Lora Wildenthal 104
Humanitarianism in Postcolonial Contexts: Some West European Examples from the 1960s to the 1980s

Contributors 123

To Stefan Kleinwächter.

Table of Contents

Eva Bischoff and Elisabeth Engel 3
Colonialism and Beyond: Race and Migration from a Postcolonial Perspective

Olaf Stieglitz 20
Bodies in Motion: Writing Sport History as a History of Modern Bodies

Robert Júlio Decker 33
White Subjects, Governmentality, and Immigration Restriction in the United States, 1894-1924

Judith Schachter 53
Sovereignty, Identity, and Indigeneity: The Case of Hawai'i

Serhat Karakayali 72
Subject Citizen: The Ambiguity of Citizenship and its Colonial Laboratories

Manuela Bojadžijev 85
Connecting Some Dots: Migration, Colonialism, and Questions of Citizenship in Postcolonial Europe

Lora Wildenthal 104
Humanitarianism in Postcolonial Contexts: Some West European Examples from the 1960s to the 1980s

Contributors 123

Colonialism and Beyond: Race and Migration from a Postcolonial Perspective

Eva Bischoff and Elisabeth Engel

"I think we need to remember that the game has changed."[1] With these words, Paul Gilroy, author of eminent studies on the history of the *Black Atlantic* or Britain's *Postcolonial Melancholia*, summarized the need for a new awareness of issues of migration, race, and discrimination at the beginning of the twenty-first century. Speaking at a Public Meeting at the North London Community House in the wake of the riots that had raged in Liverpool, Birmingham, Manchester, Bristol, and London in August 2011, Gilroy referred to the often made comparison between the race riots in 1981 and the most recent outbreaks of violence in summer 2011.

He claimed that, despite obvious similarities, there are several significant differences between the condition of migrants in British urban areas thirty years ago and their situation today. The first difference he mentioned is the establishment of a "*securitocracy*," which rules through new technologies (DNA tests, CCTV coverage of public space) and a post 9/11 anti-terrorist legislation which resulted in an increasing criminalization and incarceration of people of color.[2] In light of these changes, it cannot be considered a coincidence that the violence broke out after a demonstration in commemoration of Mark Duggan, a resident of Tottenham (North London) who had been killed during a police raid on August 4, 2011.

The second new aspect Gilroy mentioned is a profound shift in the "relationship between *information* and *power*." Whereas on the one hand, social networks such as *Twitter* or *Facebook* during August 2011 had been used by both looters and community members who wanted to defend their neighborhood from arson and vandalism, the increasing "digitalization" and "privatization" of the media during the previous years resulted in "a much tighter control over what can be said."[3] The distressing results of this development became visible to the public eye just before the riots broke out. In July 2011 the British public was confronted with facts indicating a close personal interconnectedness and political collaboration between the British Conservative Party, Prime Minister David Cameron, and Rupert Murdoch's News Corporation.[4] This form of media control found an eerie resonance in Cameron's considerations to bar suspected participants of the uprisings from access to social networks.

The third aspect Gilroy discussed in his presentation is the rapid and radical transformation of the migrant community in Britain resulting from several simultaneous developments: First, the "loss of experience" and "the loss of the imagination" as activists and intellectuals today are often selling their "services as consultants and managers and diversity trainers" instead of supporting communities and political efforts. Second, the establishment of a Black middle class. Third, the development of political Islam, and fourth the increasing numbers of migrants from Africa and Eastern Europe to the UK. Thus, he concluded, "the riots are no longer just a black-and-white story." Instead, it is a story "complicated by all kinds of changes in our cities and our communities."[5]

By raising these issues, Gilroy not only pleas for taking a close look at the locally and temporally specific situation of migrant communities in Britain, as a neo-liberal, post-racist, multiculturalist society. Also, he challenges central premises of postcolonial critique, in that they fail to acknowledge problems like securitocracy, multimedia networking and the changed composition of migrant communities as symptoms of an imperial melancholia and a new tendency to glorify the British Raj.[6] Generally speaking, all these aspects are closely related to questions of identity, racism, and the "challenges of a post-colonial world,"[7] in other words, stockpile items of postcolonial theory's crafts and trade. But this statement reflects only part of the truth. As the example of contemporary Britain demonstrates, a number of questions arise, which point at the limits of postcolonial theory as it has been developed so far: How does postcolonialism as a critical intellectual project integrate the political implications of globalization and the "war on terror" into the picture of imperial power-formations? Are the classic concepts such as "hybridity" and "nomadism" still appropriate to grasp the complexities of mobility and identity in so-called post-racist societies? From what political and intellectual location do postcolonial scholars speak today?

An increasing number of critics forcefully engage these questions. Their contributions call for a repositioning of central categories of postcolonial thinking. Yet, critical self-reflexivity is not adverse to postcolonial theory. On the contrary, postcolonialism was always far from being a homogenous field of research. To use the words of Robert Young, it is a multivocal, collective work, which "comprises [...] a related set of perspectives, which are juxtaposed against one another, on occasion contradictorily."[8] What exactly then, is novel about the current wave of critique? Is it merely a new episode of elaborate academic banter or does it introduce a fresh perspective, a new level of inquiry? How to think about race and migration from a postcolonial perspective at the beginning of the twenty-first century?

Earlier assessments of the achievements and failures of the analytical potential of postcolonial theory typically concentrated on the position of postcolonial studies within the academy in general and within English departments in particular. Another stressed the priviledged position of prominent individual thinkers such as Homi K. Bhabha and Gayatri Chakravorty Spivak.[9] Additionally, scholars such as Crystal Bartolovich, Neil Lazarus, Benita Perry, Arif Dirlik, Ella Shohat, or Ajjiz Ahmad admonished the increasing reliance on poststructuralist philosophy in postcolonial thinking while abandoning a more grounded historical and materialist critique.[10] In the words of Anita Parry:

> [I]t remains important to urge more historically grounded directions and greater discrimination in the enquiries of an ecumenical and proliferating field where the material impulses to colonialism, its appropriation of physical resources, exploitation of human labour and institutional repression, have receded from view.[11]

The most powerful among the recent critical voices build on this line of argument and combine it with a perspective which is informed by the political and social experiences of a globalized, post 9/11 world. Their arguments coalesce around the same aspects Gilroy discussed in his reflections of the British riots in summer 2011, namely the connection between capitalism and migration, the role of the body in (post-)racist societies and the necessity for historical and spatial specificity in postcolonial analyses. Taken together, the new impulses of this debate serve as a guide to the chapters of this volume, because they not only help to survey the various forms of race and migration, but also to illuminate the various ways in which the two frequently articulate each other.[12]

I. Migration and Capitalism

To undermine the seemingly stable and clear binaries of the Manichean world of colonialism, postcolonial thinkers systematically focus on reconstructing the ambivalences and ambiguities in the process of the articulation of cultural (ethnic, gender, etc.) identities. Many studies have been devoted to the development of analytical concepts to embrace the complexities of these processes. The most prominent contribution to these efforts is Homi K. Bhabha's study on the *Location of Culture*.[13] He called for a "move away from the singularities of 'class' or 'gender' as primary conceptual and organizational categories" and emphasized the necessity to "think beyond narratives of originary and initial subjectivities and to focus on those moments or processes that are produced in the articulation of cultural differences."[14]

From Bhabha's perspective, the privileged starting point to investigate the articulation of identities is the boundary, more specifically, the "interstices," the "in-between" or the "third space" that open up in situations of cultural translation. Accordingly, his deliberations (as the ones of other postcolonial thinkers) evolve around the figure of the migrant (also: the nomad) and phenomena of diasporic communities.[15] It is assumed that the "development of diasporic cultures" and their presence, as for instance those resulting from the migration to the United Kingdom from the territories of its former colonies, "necessarily questions essentialist models" and destabilizes "the ideology of a unified, 'natural' cultural norm, one that underpins the centre/margin model of colonialist discourse."[16]

This approach, however, is heavily criticized for neglecting the "miserable plight" and the harsh realities of the life of a "postmodern nomad," in particular regarding what it means "to be homeless, wandering, a refugee, following not a dream of disembodied bliss but a slim hope for survival."[17] Although part of the traditional materialist critique of the prevalence of postmodernist thinking in postcolonial theory,[18] this neglect gained unprecedented virulence in light of the escalating level of violence that is exercised to uphold border regimes at the edges of post-industrialized countries, i.e. the European Union (EU), Australia, and the United States. With regard to the EU border alone, the situation is grave.

Migrants, who try to enter the EU unregistered, die in cargo containers, drown in rivers or seas, are shot, hunted down, harassed, economically and often also sexually exploited. In the Mediterranean alone, at least 17,856 persons died along the European borders since 1988, as activist, blogger, and journalist Gabriele Del Grande reports.[19] International human rights organization such as *amnesty international* or *Pro Asyl* support his claims. Those men, women, and children who survive the ordeals and actually arrive on European soil, due to geographic proximity often on Italian territory, are treated in the most appalling manner: they are herded in so-called *Centres for Identification and Expulsion* (CIEs), and left there without proper medical care or legal advice.[20] Simultaneously, an increasing number of highly qualified business management employees and technology experts develop a migratory, nomadic lifestyle. They move within a separate, yet global sphere established by equally internationally operating private security firms, high speed networks of communication, privileged means of business class transportation and frequent flyer status.[21]

To account for these apparently disparate developments it is necessary, Robert Young argued as early as 1995, to acknowledge the double connection between nomadism/migration and capitalism. "Nomadism" he stated, is always both: a "radically anti-capitalist strategy," and a "brutal characteristic mode of capitalism itself."[22] Building on his argument, and referring to the "direct correlation between capital accumulation and proletarian misery,"[23] which becomes apparent in the plight of the refugees today, authors such as Kanishka Chowdhury, John Noyes, or Masao Miyoshi urge to address questions of migration and nomadism from a materialist perspective.[24]

They recommend two approaches: First, to acknowledge that capitalism relies on the "production of nomadic lifestyles" of both business nomads and refugees alike, while simultaneously depending "on the reintegration of these lifestyles into its own modes of production." Accordingly, they conclude, it is crucial to examine nomadism not only as "oppositional" and subversive to existing systems of exploitation but also as "integrative."[25]

Secondly, they call for an accommodation of the "brute facts of how territoriality affects lives" in postcolonial theory.[26] So far, postcolonial orthodoxy has almost exclusively concentrated on the analysis of phenomena which undermine existing national identities such as diasporic communities and "cosmopolitanism."[27] Instead of shunning the nation-state from their considerations, postcolonial scholars need to investigate it critically in its Janus-faced complexity: as a base of operations for bourgeoisie capital and apparatus of policing of migrant bodies as well as a possible site of resistance. Moreover, they need to "expose the discursive continuum between so-called diasporic, progressive narratives" and so-called "fundamentalist narratives of nation," a distinction which seems obvious only at first glance.[28] "[D]iasporic narratives are not progressive purely because they emerge from a transnational space." Instead both can and often are tied to capitalist or national interests alike. And, as Chowdhury reminds his readers, "[i]t must be the work of the postcolonial critic to reveal these relationships."[29]

II. Race and the Body

At the beginning of the twenty-first century 'race' is characterized by and constructed in a number of paradoxes. The scientific technology of genometrics, for instance, adds a molecular, and thus invisible dimension to racist profiling and discrimination, while medical treatments are significantly improved on the ground of biomolecular findings.[30] Barack Obama claimed his African-American heritage as a powerful political resource in his run for the US-presidency and acts as figurehead of a post-racist, multicultural society, while continuing the neo-colonial wars of predecessors and failing to dismantle "the shadowy, global gulag of secret interrogation prisons" as promised during his election campaign.[31] Across the Atlantic, a self-declared British multicultural society practices a form of racist profiling that is based on visual stereotypes of the Muslim 'Other' and backed by a post-9/11 and post-7/7 anti-terror legislation. Here, the nation-state, hailed by some authors as the privileged site of resistance and anti-capitalist, anti-globalization critique, acts as the architect of racist discrimination and increased policing.

Already this brief sketch of racial dynamics reveals that multiculturalism as a political project has failed to keep its promise of including everyone, including his/her cultural heritage, into the national fold. Instead, using this concept continuously re-inscribed cultural differences in an essentialist manner: in its more liberal-humanist version, it assigns habitats to every community, and in its right wing incarnation, it grouts the trenches of cultural racism. Today, an increasing number of scholars claims that the traditional concepts developed by postcolonial theory to analyze and describe the situation of migrant communities such as "hybridity" or "diaspora" in fact support the essentialist logic underlying the notion of multiculturalism instead of undermining it.[32] A critical analysis of so-called post-racist societies today, they point out, should focus on two of their central characteristics: the new politics of (in)visibility and the "Politics of Racialization."[33]

Both aspects are closely connected to the human body. The first concerns the privilege of the gaze and the enforced visibility of the 'Other.' Whereas the "imperial gaze" of earlier centuries focused exclusively on the (most often female) bodies of the colonized,[34] this new regime of (in)visibility encompasses all manifestations of human life and includes white and non-white bodies alike. It is most prevalent in the urban settings of postcolonial metropoles. Screenings, CCTV, and x-ray scanners expose all bodies to the eye of an often unseen observer who, in the name of security, can (and will) intervene in an individual's life at any point in time. The Guantánamo prison can be regarded as the heterotopia of this regime of visibility, to use a Foucauldian term. Simultaneously, this camp is a materialization of the current political strategy to remove the exertion of violence as well as the spaces in which this violence occurs from the public eye by establishing an international shadow prison system, a situation Anne McClintock has termed the "crisis of violence and the visible." It is our task as critical scholars, she continues, to expose and analyze, in other words, to render visible what the "imperial state attempts to render invisible" and focus on the "ordinary people afflicted by that violence."[35]

The second aspect, the new politics of racialization, refers even more directly to the human body and its materiality. In contrast to earlier forms of racism, which entered "the colonized through the skin," racism today "enters the colonized through paths which lie beneath the skin" as Dimitris Papadopoulos and Sanjay Sharma have pointed out in reference to Frantz Fanon. Instead of "epidermalization" or traditional racial taxonomies, we are confronted with a form of "deep essentialism" that relies on a combination of "behavioural and molecular genetics" and poses as a "double of genetic purity through ancestry, on the one hand, and social mixture through migrational movements in population genomics, on the other."[36] Additionally, as Linda Alcoff and Paul Gilroy have argued most convincingly, race and racialized identities are lived experiences. On the one hand they have sedimented into the materiality of the body itself.[37] On the other, they are strategic resources for day-to-day political and social struggles, since they have, due to the success of the civil rights movement, "turned into important sources of solidarity, joy, and collective strength."[38]

In sum, recent scholarship proposes counter-racist strategies that take into account both the level of every-day micro-processes as well as the materiality of racialized experiences. Race "is an embodied phenomenon which is felt, lived, re/made through multiple habitual ways in our everyday lives" Papadopoulos and Sharma argue and it "needs to be contested on the level where communities shift the new (biologized) meanings of race and un/do them through their everyday practices."[39] On the same note, Paul Gilroy emphasizes that, in order to overcome race and racism, we have to acknowledge that for "many racialized populations, 'race' and the hard-won, oppositional identities it supports are not to be lightly or prematurely given up" since they are intimately intertwined with individual lives and experiences. Members of "[t]hese groups will need to be persuaded very carefully that there is something worthwhile to be gained from a deliberate renunciation of 'race' as the basis for belonging to one another and acting in concert."[40]

III. Postcolonial Space|Time

There is a longstanding concern among scholars, critics and advocates of postcolonialism alike, that postcolonial theory as a set of tools for critical analysis and political change might do us a disservice. Anne McClintock has summarized these objections under the notion of the "Pitfalls of the Postcolonial."[41] "Postcolonialism," she warns, implicitly reproduces the colonial idea of "linear time and progress" by alluding to a division in before and after the historical period of colonialism.[42] Moreover, it acts as a "bogus universal" rendering geographical, political and historical differences a well as discontinuities and continuities unrecognizable: "the singular category 'postcolonial' may too readily license a panoptic tendency to view the globe through generic abstractions void of political nuance."[43] As Gilroy's remarks on the London riots in 2011 aptly demonstrate, the need for critical specificity in postcolonialism is, if that was even possible, growing.

There are two developments in recent scholarship that accommodate for this necessity. The first is the intervention of Latin American scholars, such as Enrique Dussel, Walter Mignolo or Aníbal Quijano who stress the critical potential of the "Latin American archive" that has been widely ignored by scholars in US-American and European academic contexts so far.[44] Based on the analysis of Latin American colonial experiences, these authors perceive modernity and colonialism as mutually constitutive and therefore closely intertwined.[45] This assessment of the relationship between colonialism and modernity is shared by postcolonial scholars in general. Latin American scholars, however, additionally distinguish between a *First* and a *Second Modernity*. Whereas the first "emerged during the sixteenth and seventeenth centuries and corresponds to the humanist Renaissance Christian ethos that flourished in Italy, Portugal, Spain and their respective American colonies,"[46] the second modernity, connected to the French and the British Empires, is caught in the rift between the universalistic claims of Enlightenment and racist or Orientalist discourses of the colonized 'Other.' Both modernities, however, went hand in hand with the articulation of specific subjectivities: the "ego conquiro" of the first modernity which established "an exclusionary relationship of domination" with the colonized and the "ego cogito" of the second modernity which rested upon the hierarchical racial formation of the first.[47]

This continuity notwithstanding, there are a number of particularities of Latin American *coloniality* (Quijano) in general and of the first modernity in particular that Mignolo urges us to take into account. One of the most prominent among them is the adoption and incorporation of European cultural norms and values by colonized and Creole elites alike. To describe this phenomenon he employs the term "Occidentalism" in critical reference to Said's concept of Orientalism.[48] According to Mignolo and other critics, who follow his line, Anglo-American postcolonial theory, by positioning Orientalism as the "colonial discourse par excellence [...] ends up legitimizing the eighteenth-century (Eurocentric) imaginary" of the second modernity."[49]

The second line of argument that stresses the necessity of historical specificity does so by questioning postcolonial theory as a form of *situated knowledge*, to use a term coined by Donna Haraway.[50] This critique is also an element of the intervention of the Latin American scholars mentioned above: They call for an acknowledgement of the "*colonial difference*" of each colonial formation, i.e. the "differential time-space where a particular region becomes connected to the world-system of colonial domination." From their perspective, accounting for this differential is most important on a conceptual level in order to analyze coloniality in its temporal and spacial heterogeneity but also to expose the "locus of enunciation" of postcolonial theory itself.[51] This demand is all the more urgent since they consider the invention of the objective gaze "independent of its ethnic and cultural center of observation" to be the result of the colonial expansion of the first modernity – a perspective Santiago Castro-Gómez calls "*the hubris of zero degrees*."[52] By failing to acknowledge its own locus of enunciation, traditional postcolonial theory runs the risk of reproducing this central episteme of colonial discourse.

In addition to these concerns, scholars are becoming increasingly aware of the specific historical and political context in which postcolonialism surfaced. Genealogies of postcolonial theory published so far usually locate its origin in anti-colonial struggles and the process of decolonization during the mid-twentieth century. Marxist activists such as Frantz Fanon, Aimé Césaire, and Almicar Cabral figure prominently as its intellectual ancestors.[53] Yet, this narrative obscures how strongly Postcolonialism's success as an academic field has been connected to the achievements of so-called "Third World" intellectuals, whose arrival in the British and American academy coincided with the poststructuralist turn. In the process of academic integration, postcolonialism departed from its Marxist roots and the location from which postcolonial theory used to speak which was "a precise historical intersection of Marxist political theory with Third World struggles and decolonization movements."[54] This recent critique ties in with the longstanding debate about the increasing reliance on poststructuralist theory and the neglect of a materialist approach described above.

Lastly, the recent debate about the historical location of postcolonialism introduced one other aspect worth considering: the relationship between postcolonialism and postsocialism. As scholars such as David Moore have argued, both its Marxist anti-colonial roots and its entrenchment in the Anglophone universities narrowed the focus of postcolonial studies to the former British Empire. This prevented an engagement with other imperial projects and their aftermath, such as the Russian empire and its successor, the Soviet Union.[55] Moore urges postcolonial scholarship to turn its attention to "another zone" than the imperial spaces of the Western European powers, namely "the post-Soviet sphere comprising the Baltic states, Central and Eastern Europe

[…], the Caucasus, and Central Asia" in order to finally acknowledge both "postcolonial-post-Soviet parallels" and the specificity of Russia and its history of alleged cultural inferiority in comparison to the West. Moreover, he encourages postcolonial studies and post-Soviet studies alike to establish a dialogue by using a common analytical language. So far, he states, "South does not speak East, and East not South."[56]

IV. Race and Migration from a Postcolonial Perspective

Traditionally, "postcolonial theory entails the task of 'thinking at the limits'," as Mabel Moraña, Enrique Dussel, and Carlos A. Jáuregui have emphasized in reference to the work of Stuart Hall. The "study of *coloniality*," by contrast, "implies the challenge of thinking *across* (frontiers, disciplines, territories, classes, ethnicities, epistemes, temporalities)."[57] Their observation appears even more valid against the new horizons that have been introduced in the debates mentioned above. Without claiming to make a programmatic contribution, 'thinking across' constitutes a central theme of this volume. Rather than making explicit reference to theoretical debates, the essays of this volume pursue lines of inquiry that link, contest and refine postcolonial perspectives on race and migration.

Each chapter focuses on one historically specific formation in which race and migration became mutually constituting practices. This, however, does not imply to presuppose race and migration as a binary pair of shifting relationships. Rather, each contribution addresses the question to what extent specific articulations of race and migration also help to historicize the postcolonial nation state within and beyond the spatial and temporal logic of empire. On the one hand, this approach foregrounds movements and forms of organization of non-state actors as indications of both the social, transnational spaces these moving actors created and the role of postcolonial nation states in facilitating and/or foreclosing these spaces. The interplay between mobility and non-stately agency beyond and among empires sheds new light on a number of classical questions of postcolonial studies, including citizenship, sovereignty, and racialized bodies, while it also brings into view new transnational patterns of political activism and belonging evolving along with migration movements, transnational biopolitics of whiteness or the humanitarianism of Non-Governmental Organizations (NGOs).

On the other hand, this volume uncouples the postcolonial perspective itself from its seemingly inherent focus on the bilateral relationship between colony and metropole. Following the itineraries of non-state actors onto the colonial stage means to leave the territorial boundaries of individual empires behind and to acknowledge the entire globe as their potential field of operation. In many cases, it was the actors' mobility that facilitated the exchange of imperial knowledge that provoked practices of exclusion and racialization, and that simultaneously shifted, redefined or transgressed boundaries from below. The resulting formations of race and migrations, we argue, thus speak to global entanglements structured by the (post)colonial state, without being congruent with colonial geographies or the metropole-colony logic.[58]

To illustrate these arguments, the assembled case studies pay tribute to a central feature of postcolonial studies: an interdisciplinary perspective. Interdisciplinarity enables the development of analytical tools necessary to account for the historical specificity of (post)colonial experiences, the heterogeneity of imperial spaces, and for questioning postcolonialism's own political, historical, and social locations as a mode of academic knowledge production. The ways in which intersections of race and migration were fixed, (re-)articulated and contested, as these essays show, varied widely in time and space, and touch upon topics crucial across disciplines – ranging from history, anthropology, ethnology, and political science to sociology. To give a comprehensive overview thus lies beyond the scope of this collection. It rather presents a cursory survey of potential starting points for applying postcolonial perspectives on race and migration. More significantly, it emphasizes the irreducibility of disciplinary and historical perspectives by engaging in a detailed examination of both colonial and postcolonial phenomena.

As *Olaf Stieglitz* argues, the conceptual association of mobility and modernity – established in sports history – can be expanded towards a microhistory of the modern body in motion. With the example of the 'Australian Crawl,' Stieglitz illustrates that the national myth of the 'invention' of freestyle swimming in white Australia tells the interrelated story of indigenous sporting practices of athletes from and migrating in the Pacific region. At the same time, the athlete's body became a focal point of scientific examination, entertainment industry and visual technology at the turn of the nineteenth century. From the perspective of a modern body history, sporting bodies thus appear as at once highly exposed, racialized and gendered while their movements in time and space always also transcended scientific categorization and national constraints. More than that, as Stieglitz's example demonstrates, they created alternative 'contact zones' and transnational spaces between the white settler colony of Australia and the Pacific Islands.

Judith Schachter presents another aspect of the interconnected history of the Pacific. Focusing on US legal adjustments to the relationship between Native Hawaiians and the Federal Government, Schachter illustrates the specter of postcolonial implications of Hawaiian claims to indigeneity, national identity, and sovereignty. Introduced in 2000 by Daniel Akaka, the "Native Hawaiian Government Reorganization Act" proposed steps for Native Hawaiians to gain federal recognition similar to Native Americans in the US. The Akaka Bill stood at the center of movements for Hawai`i's political autonomy and prompted ongoing controversies over the basis of Hawai`i's political unity as a nation and over the definition of Native Hawaiians as a race, tribe, or distinct native community. On a broader scale, disputes over the Bill expose the difficulties of asserting sovereignty against a history of colonialism without re-inscribing racial (self)designations shaped by the rhetoric and practices of the United States' colonial regime.

Similar practices of racial designation were crucial for the creation of the American subject-citizen already a century ago, as *Júlio Decker* demonstrates in his contribution to this volume. In the context of the 'new immigration,' gaining momentum in the early twentieth century, the perceived invasion of foreigners triggered a range of new forms of civic commitment, governmental practices and stately border and population regulation. As much as these measures targeted migration flows from Eastern and Southern Europe, they also addressed American citizens themselves. With the example of the *Immigration Restriction League*, a lobby group for restricting immigration on a racial basis, Decker shows that the emergence of 'racial American selves' got strongly linked to civic duties, a process that in turn involved the civic plea for an official definition of the 'essence of whiteness' and its defense through the state. The progressive character implied in such restrictionist endeavors thus helps to question the assumption of whiteness as an unquestioned "normality." Instead, the case of US immigration restriction reveals the intertwined struggle for creating a form of white superiority that differentiated Americans not only from Europeans, but also 'Americanized' the transnational collective of 'Anglo-Saxons.'

In line with this argument of a 'reversed vector' pointing to internal contradictions and differences within Western societies, *Serhat Karakayali* questions the laboratory paradigm predominant in colonial studies. With the example of urban planning in Northern Africa during the French colonial period, Karakayali dismantles the idea of 'laboratory conditions' as a colonial fantasy that emerged in the context of the effort to modernize the metropole rather than the colony. The architecture in North African cities, accordingly, became the object of urban planner's study, instead of the subject of modern French design. Most of all, architects examined urban slums in order to develop models for the creation of functioning social structures in settlements that were to be erected in France. The creation of worker's settlements then exposes the state's ambiguous aim to integrate workers as citizens by disciplining them within certain housing policies. Simultaneously, spatial exclusion went hand in hand with fixating biological characteristics on the working class. This form of modern class racism in Europe, as Karakayali demonstrates, carried the colonial-racist imprint of an 'internal colonization,' and reflected the tense relationship between democracy, planning and statehood in Western society, rather than colonial laboratory experiments in North Africa.

Lora Wildenthal expands the scope of colony-metropole relations towards the post-1945 era, when European NGOs began to confront the humanitarian challenges of the post-decolonization era. Drawing on the examples of *Terres des Hommes*, *Amnesty for Women*, and *Cap Anamur*, Wildenthal delineates the perspective of European 'postcolonial humanitarianism,' in order to grasp popular understandings of race, sovereignty, human rights and power. All of these organizations acted in the ideological context of the Third World debate sparked within the Left in Europe over the 1960s. While newly independent states initially figured as revolutionary inspiration, the realities of poverty, disease, sexual exploitation and refugee camps soon disenchanted the Third World project's heroic anti-colonial violence. As a result, humanitarian aid organizations subscribed to French existentialist doctrines, whose nonpolitical and anti-ideological tone expressed their deep disrespect for states, and pushed them towards taking the freedom to move between the First and the Third World on behalf of easing its sufferings. While the latter easily appears to perpetuate humanitarian gesturing of the colonial period, the agents' apparent consciousness of the illegitimacy of states and colonialism complicates the assumption of continuities. By taking humanitarians' strident claims to being non-political and non-state agents seriously, Wildenthal ultimately questions predominant assumptions about anti- and post-colonial agency.

While humanitarian aid often is directed at areas the outside of Europe, directing money, affects, and political concern to postcolonial spaces, *Manuela Bojadžijev* reminds us of a reverse movement, namely that of migrants, which in turn shaped (and continues to shape) Europe and its postcolonial condition. Focusing on Germany, a European country that only recently acknowledged its status as an immigration country, Bojadžijev explores three forms of autonomous migrant organization and solidarity networks at three different times. The case of anti-colonial activists, who lived in German metropoles such as Berlin during the 1920s and 1930 testifies to the possibility to move and organize freely across continents on behalf of the shared struggle for their home countries' liberation; the case of labor migrants, who were officially recruited by the German government during the 1960s and 1970s, demonstrates migrant efforts to independently improve their living conditions in the host country; and the case of refugees stuck in the Mediterranean Sea in 2011, whose sufferings forged the creation of solidarity networks lobbying for their immediate admission to Europe, shows that also forced migration does not come along without some form of organization. Implicit to these accounts, as Bojadžijev reveals, has been the re-definition of European borders and identities as a direct response to postcolonial migration movements. Against this background, debates on "European citizenship," which is both desired and neglected, thus emerges as a highly contested and versatile matter, rather than a legally defined status.

As indicated by this overview, the essays of this collection present theoretical considerations and research findings that are recent, preliminary, and necessarily in progress, also because each project relates to the ongoing debates/mapping of the limits and opportunities of postcolonial scholarship. In their entirety, they might contribute to generating a set of new lines of inquiry that draws attention to research topics that formerly lay beyond the classical scope of postcolonial studies.

Simultaneously, each chapter of this volume represents the proceedings of the *Brown Bag Lecture Series* at the University of Cologne in spring 2009.

This lecture series came into being due to the intellectual curiosity of a group of people, students and junior researchers alike, who are interested in British, German, and American History written from a postcolonial perspective. Our collection here documents one of many inspiring lecture series organized by this group. We have the honor and the privilege to publish this volume, but both the series and the book would have been impossible without the courage and dedication of all those wonderful people, whose names do not appear on the front page. Many thanks to: Rahab Njeri, Christoph Laugs, Thomas Meier, Gauri Sarang, Alexander Bräuer, Isabella Potter, Daniel Farynski, and Steffi Büttner. Additionally we would like to thank Sophie Perl, Julius Wilm, Nicole Kvale, Kimberly Dawn Waters, David Juliano, and Nina Schweisthal for their generous help. The publication of this volume is kindly supported by the Gender Equality Office of the *John F. Kennedy Institute for North American Studies*, Freie Universität Berlin.

Notes:

[1] Blog the dream of safety, "Paul Gilroy Speaks on the Riots, August 2011, Tottenham, North London," 16 August 2011, reporting on Gilroy's speech at the Public Meeting at North London Community House, 22 Moorefield Rd, London, on 15 August 2011, entitled "After the Riots… Defend our Young People, Give them a Future," http://dreamofsafety. blogspot.com (accessed 21 Oct. 2012).
[2] Ibid.
[3] Ibid.
[4] For recent information as well as a timeline of events see BBC "News: Phone-Hacking Scandal," http://www.bbc.co.uk/news/uk-14045952 (accessed 21 Oct. 2012).
[5] Blog the dream of safety, "Paul Gilroy Speaks on the Riots".
[6] As one of the most prominent examples for the latter see Niall Ferguson, Empire. How Britain Made the Modern World (London: Penguin Books, 2004). A critical reflection on current public debates on "Britain's imperial record" can be found in Elizabeth Buettner, "'Setting the Record Straight'? Imperial History in Postcolonial British Public Culture," in Hybrid Cultures, Nervous States. Britain and Germany in a (Post)Colonial World, eds. Ulrike Lindner, Maren Stroh, Mark Stein and Silke Stroh (Amsterdam: Rodopi, 2010), 89-104, 89.
[7] Bill Ashcroft, Gareth Griffiths and Helen Tiffin, The Empire Writes Back. Theory and Practice in Post-colonial Literatures (New York: Routledge, 2002 [1989]), i.
[8] Robert Young, Postcolonialism. A Very Short Introduction (Oxford: Oxford University Press, 2003), 6-7. Scholars such as Graham Huggan accordingly distinguish between "first" and "second wave" postcolonialism. According to

Huggan, the first evolved from literary criticism, the latter opened its perspective to a "culturally oriented analysis." Graham Huggan, Interdisciplinary Measures. Literature and the Future of Postcolonial Studies (Liverpool: University Press, 2008), 10, 12. This is, however, not a differentiation we would like to pursue here. Rather we would like to point at a specific *urgence* to rethink postcolonial categories in the light of the most recent developments in post 9/11, 'postracist' societies.

[9] This intrinsically academic line of argument continues until today. John Hawley, for instance, suggests – after elaborately summarizing the different voices of criticism so far – to include non-English speaking literatures, questions of genre, and the perspective of queer studies to revive the withering field of postcolonialism. John Hawley, "The Colonizing Impulse of Postcolonial Theory," MFS Modern Fiction Studies 56,4 (2010): 769-87.

[10] Crystal Bartolovich and Neil Lazarus, eds., Marxism, Modernity and Postcolonial Studies (Cambridge: Cambridge University Press, 2002); Benita Parry, Postcolonial Studies. A Materialist Critique (New York: Routledge, 2004); Arif Dirlik, "The Postcolonial Aura. Third World Criticism in the Age of Global Capitalism," Critical Inquiry 20,2 (1994): 328-56; Ella Shohat, "Notes on the 'Post-Colonial'," Social Text 31/32 (1992): 99-113; Aijaz Ahmad, In Theory. Classes, Nations, Literatures (London: Verso, 2000 [1992]).

[11] Parry, Postcolonial Studies, 3.

[12] We are, for practical reasons, excluding one other aspect from further inquiry here, namely the current debate on violence, terror, and the postcolonial. See for instance Elleke Boehmer and Stephen Morton, eds., Terror and the Postcolonial. A Concise Companion (Malden: Wiley-Blackwell, 2010); Derek Gregory and Allan Pred, eds., Violent Geographies. Fear, Terror, and Political Violence (New York: Routledge, 2007).

[13] Homi K. Bhabha, The Location of Culture. With a New Preface by the Author (New York: Routledge, 2010 [1994]).

[14] Ibid., 2.

[15] Ibid., 2, 10-11, 53-6. Robin Cohen's work, although he is not necessarily a postcolonial thinker, has been most influential in this context. Robin Cohen, Global Diasporas. An Introduction (New York: Routledge, 2008 [1997]).

[16] Bill Ashcroft, Gareth Griffiths and Helen Tiffin, Post-colonial Studies. The Key Concepts (New York: Routledge, 2000), 70.

[17] John K. Noyes, "Nomadism, Nomadology, Postcolonialism. By Way of Introduction," Interventions. International Journal of Postcolonial Studies 6,2 (2004): 159-68.

[18] See for example Benita Parry, "Problems in Current Theories of Colonial Discourse," Oxford Literary Review 9,1 (1987): 27-58 and Ahmad, In Theory. See also Epifanio San Juan, Beyond Postcolonial Theory (New York: St. Martin's Press, 1999).

[19] Gabriele Del Grande, Blog Fortress Europe, http://www.fortresseurope.blogspot.com (accessed 21 Oct. 2012).
[20] Gabriele del Grande, Das Meer zwischen uns. Flucht und Migration in Zeiten der Abschottung, ed. by borderline europe e.V. and Pro Asyl e.V. (Karlsruhe: Von-Loeper-Literaturverlag, 2011), 150-81.
[21] One might also argue that many postcolonial thinkers themselves, G.C. Spivak being the most obvious example, belong to this group of elite nomads who are pursuing political projects on both the local and the global level. Still, in contrast to business advisors and technology experts who often have European or American passports, activists from the Global South are subjected to racist border regimes.
[22] Robert J. C. Young, Colonial Desire. Hybridity in Theory, Culture, and Race (New York: Routledge, 2006 [1995]), 172-3. See also Masao Miyoshi, "A Borderless World? From Colonialism to Transnationalism and the Decline of the Nation-State," Critical Inquiry 19,4 (1993): 726-51 (reprinted in: Diana Brydon, ed., Postcolonialism. Critical Concepts in Literary and Cultural Studies, Vol. 5 (New York: Routledge, 2001), 1867-92).
[23] Kanishka Chowdhury, "Interrogating 'Newness'. Globalization and Postcolonial Theory in the Age of Endless War," Cultural Critique 62,1 (2006): 126-61, 147.
[24] Noyes, "Nomadism, Nomadology, Postcolonialism," 166-7; Chowdhury, "Interrogating 'Newness'," 146-7.
[25] Noyes, "Nomadism, Nomadology, Postcolonialism," 166.
[26] Ibid., 159.
[27] Anthony Appiah, Cosmopolitanism. Ethics in a World of Strangers (New York: Norton, 2007 [2006]).
[28] Chowdhury, "Interrogating 'Newness'," 153.
[29] Ibid. 154.
[30] A feminist voice on this development: Anne Fausto-Sterling, "The Bare Bones of Sex. Part 1 – Sex and Gender," Signs 30,2 (2005): 1491-1527.
[31] Anne McClintock, "Paranoid Empire. Specters from Guantánamo and Abu Ghraib," Small Axe 28,13/1 (2009): 50-74, 51.
[32] Dimitris Papadopoulos and Sanjay Sharma, "Editorial. Race/Matter – Materialism and the Politics of Racialization," darkmatter 2, 23 Feb. 2008, http://www.darkmatter101.org/site/2008/02/23/racematter-materialism-and-the-politics-of-racialization (accessed 21 Oct. 2012). An argument that we already see in Michael Hardt's and Antonio Negri's study Empire (Cambridge, Mass: Harvard University Press, 2000), 137-8, 143-6.
[33] Papadopoulos and Sharma, "Editorial. Race/Matter."
[34] Ann E. Kaplan, Looking for the Other. Feminism, Film and the Imperial Gaze (New York: Routledge, 1996); Kirsten Fischer, "The Imperial Gaze. Native American, African American, and Colonial Women in European Eyes,"

in A Companion to American Women's History, ed. Nancy A. Hewitt (Oxford: Blackwell, 2007 [2005]), 1-19.

[35] McClintock, "Paranoid Empire," 52. See also Derek Gregory, "Vanishing Points. Law, Violence, and Exception in the Global War Prison," in Terror and the Postcolonial. A Concise Companion, eds. Elleke Boehmer and Stephen Morton (Malden: Wiley-Blackwell, 2010), 55-98.

[36] Papadopoulos and Sharma, "Editorial. Race/Matter."

[37] Linda Martin Alcoff, "Towards a Phenomenology of Racial Embodiment," Radical Philosophy 95 (1999): 15-24.

[38] Paul Gilroy, Between Camps. Nations, Cultures and the Allure of Race (New York: Routledge, 2004 [2000]), 12.

[39] Papadopoulos and Sharma, "Editorial. Race/Matter."

[40] Gilroy, Between Camps, 12.

[41] Anne McClintock, Imperial Leather. Race, Gender and Sexuality in the Colonial Contest (New York: Routledge, 1995), 9.

[42] Ibid., 10.

[43] Ibid., 11. She also argues that by recentering global history around the history European expansion, colonialism returns the moment it disappeared. Whether or not European colonialism ever disappeared is subject to intense debate in the face of contemporary US hegemony and the "war on terror."

[44] Mabel Moraña, Enrique Dussel and Carlos A. Jáuregui, "Colonialism and Its Replicants," in Coloniality at Large. Latin America and the Postcolonial Debate, eds. eid. (Durham: Duke University Press, 2008), 1-20, 4.

[45] Walter D. Mignolo, Local Histories/Global Designs. Coloniality, Subaltern Knowledges, and Border Thinking (Princeton: Princeton University Press, 2000), 17-8; Walter D. Mignolo, The Darker Side of the Renaissance. Literacy, Territoriality, and Colonization (Ann Arbor: University of Michigan Press, 2003 [1995]), vii.

[46] Santiago Castro-Gómez, "(Post)Coloniality for Dummies. Latin American Perspectives on Modernity, Coloniality, and the Geopolitics of Knowledge," in Coloniality at Large, eds. Moraña, Dussel and Jáuregui, 259-85, 272.

[47] Castro-Gómez, "(Post)Coloniality for Dummies," 273.

[48] Mignolo, Local Histories/Global Designs, 57-60; Mignolo, Darker Side, 323-6.

[49] Castro-Gómez, "(Post)Coloniality for Dummies," 277.

[50] Donna Haraway, "Situated Knowledges. The Science Question in Feminism and the Privilege of Partial Perspective," Feminist Studies 14,3 (1988): 575-99. See also Davinder P. S. Ahluwalia, Out of Africa. Post-Structuralism's Colonial Roots (New York: Routledge, 2010).

[51] Moraña, Dussel and Jáuregui, "Colonialism and Its Replicants", 6 (emphasis in the original). See also Walter D. Mignolo, "I Am Where I Think. Epistemology and the Colonial Difference," Journal of Latin American Cultural Studies 8,2 (1999): 235-45; Mignolo, Local Histories/Global Designs, 273-7.

[52] Castro-Gómez, "(Post)Coloniality for Dummies," 278 (emphasis in the original).

[53] Robert Young, Postcolonialism. An Historical Introduction (Malden: Blackwell, 2011 [2001]), 1-11, 159-334; Ania Loomba, Colonialism/ Postcolonialism (New York: Routledge, 2010 [1998]), 22-41; John McLeod, Beginning Postcolonialism (Manchester: Manchester University Press, 2010), 19-25.

[54] Timothy Brennan, "Postcolonial Studies between the European Wars. An Intellectual History," in Marxism, Modernity and Postcolonial Studies, eds. Bartolovich and Lazarus, 185-203. See also Chowdhury, "Interrogating 'Newness'", 133 and San Juan, Beyond Postcolonial Theory, 10.

[55] David Chioni Moore, "Is the Post- in Postcolonial the Post- in Post-Soviet? Toward a Global Postcolonial Critique," PMLA 116,1 (2001): 111-28.

[56] Moore, "Is the Post- in Postcolonial," 115.

[57] Moraña, Dussel and Jáuregui, "Colonialism and Its Replicants," 16-7 (emphasis in the original).

[58] Ann Laura Stoler, Carole McGranahan and Peter C. Perdue, Imperial Formations (Santa Fe, N.M.: School for Advanced Research Press, 2007).

Bodies in Motion: Writing Sport History as a History of Modern Bodies

Olaf Stieglitz

I.

In 1901, a teenager arrives from the Solomon Islands in Sydney, Australia. The boy's name is Alick Wickham, and shortly after this arrival he takes part in a swimming contest held in the Sydney harbor. The audience cheers with enthusiasm, not only because Wickham wins by a large margin but also because of his remarkable, never before seen swimming style that combined a rotating arm stroke with a parallel kick of both legs; something called the 'scissor-kick' later on. On the shore, a then well-known coach watched young Alick's astonishing speed and his continuous movements through the water and shouted excitingly: "Look at that kid crawling!"

That is, summarized in a few brief words, the founding myth of what became known as the 'Australian Crawl,' a very early variant of what today is called freestyle in competitive swimming. In the years afterwards, the 'Australian Crawl' was systematically studied, refined, trained and nationally claimed to form the basis of Australia's fame as a records-breaking, medals-winning swimming power. As with all myths, it is not entirely invented but serves as a cultural narrative which emphasizes certain aspects of the story while neglecting others. This will become evident when looking at the more complex story as researched by Australian historians Gary Osmond and Murray Phillips, in whose texts one can read more thoroughly about this episode and its meaning.[1]

In fact, in the years before Wickham arrived in Sydney, competitive swimming had become an enormously popular spectator sport. Starting in the late nineteenth century, the press on Australia's east coast discussed reports about very capable swimmers among the Pacific Islanders. They emphasized how these swimmers employed certain body movements – named *tuppa ta pala* in the indigenous language – which were completely different from the various forms of breaststrokes thought to be common among people from European descent. The style seen on the islands stimulated experimentation. A handful of swimmers, from British descent, used the rotating arm stroke, but stuck to the frog-like leg kick characteristic of breaststroke swimming. In other words, Alick Wickham was not the first to 'crawl,' he merely added another element to a complex body movement and was capable of doing so over the entire distance of a 66 and 2/3 yards junior race. The enthusiastic reaction of the bystanding coach is nowhere documented in any primary source.

Alick Wickham (1886-1967), was the son of an English merchant who had married a wife from the Solomon Islands. His career was successful, and the Australian press, with ongoing jubilation, referred to him as "the dusky lad from the Islands." Articles on Wickham and his successes continued to appear for years.[2] In 1913, a journalist characterized and authenticated his style as "nature's stroke, handed down to him from his forefathers."[3] Another writer called the new style "much neater and graceful" than any other way of swimming.[4] At about this time, the Australian-crawl-foundation-myth started to build up, and it came into full existence in 1929, when another coach, Dudley Hellmrich, published the official handbook of the *Australian Swimming Association* entitled *How to Swim.*[5] Not only a manual that teaches several swimming techniques, the book also functioned as a national history of swimming. In a chapter with the heading "Origin of the Crawl," Hellmrich tells – for the first time, it seems – the story of Wickham's premiere race in the Sydney harbor and how the watching coach shouted the famous line: "Look at that kid crawling!" Moreover, he prominently underscores Wickham's origin from the Pacific Islands, whose inhabitants he describes as natural swimmers and watermen, and as "nimble savages" – a topos that dates back to the first travel accounts by James Cook and other South Sea explorers. But this positive evaluation of Islanders in terms of physicality, exoticness and romanticized innocence was only one side of contemporary Australia's characterization of Pacific Islanders. In their declared effort to build a 'White Australia,' they were part of a complex web of race relations. The way from the *tuppa ta pala* to the 'Australian Crawl' is a tiny element of that overall story of inventing, building, and establishing the Australian nation: the colonization and whitening of what was perceived or imagined as an indigenous body movement. After the First World War, the crawl, the fastest way of swimming, had become a trademark of the new nation, it had won her medals at Olympic Games, and it had put Sydney onto the international map as a kind of world's capital of swimming.[6]

At about the same time, another Australian, Annette Kellerman (1887-1975), became an international sport star, too.[7] At age fifteen, she won her first regional swimming title and also participated in diving contests. As was the case with Wickham, traveling was both condition and result of her prominence and her influence. In 1905, at age eighteen, Kellerman traveled to Europe and swam river races in London and Paris against male competitors. She also became the first women to try – three times and always unsuccessfully – to swim the English Channel. After that she moved to the United States in order to become a professional athlete, a vaudeville dancer and a Hollywood star. But initially, her performances were scandalized – in 1907, she was arrested in Boston charged with 'indecent exposure' because she was wearing one of her self-created, one-piece swimming suits and further shows were forbidden. Some sources state that Kellerman actually provoked her arrest to arouse publicity to her new fashion line of bathing outfits, but the truth of these allegations remains uncertain.[8] Although swimming was on the one hand among the few sports at that time where competition was considered appropriate for women – since 1912 it was even part of the program of the newly re-invented, modern Olympic Games –, concerns regarding the display of certain body parts that were considered too private (legs, for instance) were still widespread. On the other hand, Kellerman's body and her sport activities became the object of scientific discourse. They were useful references for both sides in the ongoing dispute among physical education experts as to whether the muscular bodies of female athletes were undermining Victorian standards of respectability and modesty, or whether they were valuable assets in the eugenic battle to save the white race and ensure its survival. In a 1910 *New York Times* article, Dr. Dudley A. Sargent, a scholar from *Harvard University's Medical School* and author of several books on health and physical education, sided with the latter argument and dubbed Kellerman "the Perfect Woman" with regard to her balanced body proportions and her overall fitness.[9] Besides her athletic performances and her fashion designing, Kellerman was also a dancer, did water ballet and is currently considered one of the people who inspired what is now known as synchronized swimming. Such a multi-talent made Hollywood interested, and when in the early 1910s Kellerman first appeared in aquatic adventure movies (with titles such as *The Mermaid*, *Neptune's Daughter* or *Venus of the South Sea*, and unfortunately most of them are considered lost today) the display of her body became even more widespread and culturally present. Hence, the successful athlete Annette Kellerman was equally famous as a beauty, a self-promoter, a film star and a fitness guru – an early twentieth-century mixture of Elle McPherson, Madonna, Nicole Kidman and Jane Fonda – as one scholar recently stated.[10] At that time, the images of her body in motion were an emblem, a transnational reference for discussing the modern white female body, the body of the 'new woman,' its proper appearance and scientific development, its capabilities and limits.

II.

How is the modern body characterized, what makes bodies *the* location to produce and discuss specifically modern layers of meaning? Two quotations might serve as guides in a helpful direction. Neither originate – and that should be considered important – in the field of sport per se, but from the worlds of business and creative writing/intellectual life, respectively. The first one is taken from a success manual for managers, written by management advisor Katherine Blackford and published in New York, 1916. Talking about the "Man of Bone and Muscle" she says:

> This man loves motion. He is not satisfied with slow, languid motion, but he demands speed, greater and ever greater speed. […] This man drives his steamship at thirty knots an hour, his locomotives at 70 miles an hours, his automobiles at 100, and his aeroplanes at 120. He is setting higher and yet higher records for running, leaping, swimming, rowing, throwing weights, and driving horses. [His actions, O.S.] are being constantly studied, constantly improved, and constantly raised to higher and higher performances in speed of production, speed of transportation, speed of accomplishment. This man not only demands speed,

> but he demands space. The man who can travel at a hundred miles an hour needs many hundred miles in which to travel.[11]

Fifteen years later, in 1931, Erika Mann, the oldest daughter of the writer Thomas Mann and an enthusiastic car race participant, wrote in an essay published in a Berlin magazine named *Tempo*:

> If you want to try someone out – Lady or Gentlemen – neither go to the theatre, nor dancing – do some traveling, some sporting traveling, go skiing with that person to be tested or, even better, drive in an automobile. Nothing discloses more, nothing unveils more of one's character than doing sports [...] Sport alone can show it.[12]

Two quotations, one and a half decades, one world war and an ocean apart, but both demonstrate how reference to the moving body in time and space, to sport and physical culture had become part of the overall socio-cultural setting of 'western' nations experiencing a highly dynamic process of modernization. Notions of movement in time and space, of acceleration and of the importance of measuring speed, distance and accomplishment are crucial elements in a modernity that builds on sciences that discuss smallest elements in constant oscillations, a modernity that builds on ergonomics measuring human physical motions and analyzing them according to the needs of ever faster running machines, a modernity in which images start to move and that depict moving human beings on machines in motion. With new techniques of serial photography and then film (the movies, as they were called), the representation of the body/bodies in motion advanced to the core of modernity's cultural production. Next to animals, it was the sporting human body on which the analytic eye of the camera focused.[13] The well-known cards by Eadweard Muybridge may serve as an example, as well as the many sport films produced by the companies of Thomas Edison and other entrepreneurs. Eugen Sandow, whom Ralph Poole named the first male pin-up model, and various boxing champions became objects of desire for the audiences of cinema that generated its sensation and its ability in attracting large crowds of people just because they were displaying images of moving bodies.[14]

Moreover, in this moment of disenchanting the human body through science and technology, the modern self was formed and formed itself most prominently along attributes that focused on ideas of 'natural bodies.' Additionally, stratifying and regulating modern societies rested very much on physical attributes and forms of subjectivation bound upon seemingly stable physical categories such as gender, race, ethnicity, or age. Among those social practices responsible for transmitting, charging and essentializing these ideas, sport rapidly and increasingly gained crucial prominence: sport mobilized, produced and constantly displayed bodies in motion. This practice continues today.

Not only with regard to Australia and competitive swimming, but also in many other parts of the world, sport and physical leisure activities became enormously popular from the late nineteenth century onward. At that time, what we now consider sport came into existence in a truly modern design. Modern sport was characterized by a set of features.[15]

First of all, sport became a class-transgressing mass phenomenon, both with regard to practicing and watching sport. Along with this development came a trend of specialization, professionalization and commercialization of sport on all levels, a process that facilitated sport's capacity to form individual and collective subjects. Sport reached beyond the playing field or the gymnasium, it created its own media and produced mutual relations to advertising, fashion and commerce.

Furthermore, the emergence of modern sport was closely linked to dominant discourses of scientific racism and social Darwinism. As such, it coincided with the establishment of a biopolitical order underscoring the systematic management, fostering and cultivation of populations. Individual bodies, declared strong, healthy and capable of reproduction, were supposed to morph into a superior collective body that should be 'healthy,' 'fit,' and 'pure.' At this point, ideas about a biologically determined development of societies as well as their inner stratification merged with notions of performance, competition and success in sport, a social practice more and more considered valuable in achieving this objective. In order to classify and stratify bodies along lines of gender, race, health, and ability, sport became a powerful instrument – where else is 'doing gender' or 'doing race' more publicly on display?

Modern sport moreover advanced the 'truth' of social stratification and hierarchy, for it actively linked performance and success to bodily attributes. Success and failure in sport signified certain positions in society, labeled individuals and groups along biological determined categories. The reverse was also true: these hierarchical social positions and these biological markers decided who was able to take part in sporting activities, actively or passively, which behavior was socially accepted and which was not. In other words: Sport regulated who was allowed to become a subject.

As a result of these trends, sport and surrounding fields of physical culture became increasingly part of scientific discourse. A desire to optimize performances, to win with a new record, corresponded with analyzing and regulating training, diet and life style and was combined with motion studies, body measurements and other bio-medical (and pharmacological) interventions.

With regard to organization, clubs and associations were established on the local, regional, national and international levels. Both professional and amateur leagues as well as championships were founded. Pierre de Coubertin reinvented the Olympic Games, and along with them an international movement that constituted as much a critique on nationalism as it was part of that project. An ethic of equality called for fair play on the field and in the arena, again reinforcing notions of stable differences between persons considered not equal enough to compete against each other – male and female bodies, for instance.

Finally, modern sport was from its beginnings inextricably linked to ever changing media constellations. The development of certain sports and certain forms of media were often strongly interrelated – film, for example, during the 1900s and 1910s was very successfully promoted through representing boxing bouts which in themselves had to be adapted to the conditions of a new technology that needed daylight. "Covering sports in the media," in the words of the editors of a recent anthology, "must not be understood as merely a form of discursive duplication of some 'true event.'"[16] Modern sport in this sense is always a mediated practice.

To put it another way, rephrased as a scholarly program: If it's true that the processes of forming modern societies and modern subjects are to a large degree structured by underlying aspects usually attributed to the body, like gender, race, ethnicity, or age, then sport and physical culture are perhaps *the* bodily practices to look at. Sport is one cultural practice, where 'doing gender' and 'doing race' were practiced in the truest sense of these phrases. Where, if not in modern sport activities, were bodies and the attributes attached to them more clearly presented, measured, categorized, labeled, contrasted, played with and sensationalized? In sport, bodies became a widely recognized and highly visible interface of blueprints for race and gender, for ideas about youth and age in general, for stating ability and declaring disability, for celebrating notions of beauty and health and stigmatizing the abject, for both individual and collective images of the self and of others. Watching and analyzing a prizefight, a soccer match, a hurdles race or a competition in synchronized swimming tell something about how a given society is organized, tell something about stratification and hierarchies, about inclusion and exclusion, and tell something about tradition, change and cultural memory. All this sounds too obvious, and for this reason it is the more surprising that, first, sport history seems not to be very interested in the cultural turn of the humanities; and, second, cultural history does not deal with sport and physical culture to a very large extent either.

III.

In 1991, the British sport historian Tony Mason stated that sport history has been largely written by what he called "fans with typewriters."[17] Even at that point in time, this was meant simultaneously as self-irony and provocation. Since then, the overall outlook of sport history has profoundly changed. In a somewhat belated adoption of the historiographical paradigm of social history, the field gained in reputation and acceptance, although it still remained at the margins of both 'general history' on the one hand and sport studies on the other, which as a project originating in Cold War thinking always emphasized sport medicine, biomechanics or the methodology of training over historical or sociological approaches that were not especially helpful in gaining prestigious medals at Olympics. So the field was touched by the cultural turn only a few years ago, also belatedly, and as in so many areas questions of gender proved to be a crucial, most valuable catalyst in leading the way. For, according to Patricia Vertinsky, a Canadian historian and one of the leading protagonists of the newer sport history, "gender is the way bodies are drawn into history; bodies are arenas for the making of gender patterns."[18]

Vertinsky attributes an enormous potential to a gendered historiography of sport that accentuates interrelation and intersection, which looks at power relations not only between women and men, but also in-between different conceptions of femininity and masculinity, and that highlights gendered bodies in their ever changing relations to other categories of identity construction like race, age, or class. The numbers of studies that follow her suggestions are increasing steadily for some years now, inspired by an overall discussion about critical race theory and analyzing ever changing notions of blackness and whiteness. Postcolonial theory also proved to be influential, not only in the chronological and spatial senses of the term, but also in analyzing the roles and prominence of sport for both colonizers and colonized, for colonizing and seeking liberation and independence. Even more importantly, the epistemological implications of postcolonial theory, of a certain worldview based on notions of intertwined metropolis and periphery, guided some newer publications on sport history.[19]

But it also remains true what Uta Andrea Balbier criticized in a research survey she published in 2005 in *Archiv für Sozialgeschichte.*[20] As she demonstrates, most publications still operate in a conceptional frame basically inspired by traditional conventions of political history and that focus on national and/or international institutions as collective singulars. Cultural history remains largely limited to questions of how sport and national identity politics correlate. The actual bodies actively involved in sport and physical culture thus remain largely out of the picture, an aspect also pointed out by the editors of *WerkstattGeschichte* in their special issue on the history of sport that was published in 2006.[21] Still, if one is willing to look from a different perspective, inspiring studies are all over the place, in the histories of the body and of sexuality modeled after the ideas of Michel Foucault and others, and in a new wave of sport sociology that does not restrict itself to counting members of clubs but asks for the meaning of physical culture and the body in our postmodern societies.[22]

So the inspiration originates not so much in classical sport history but is stimulated by the cultural turn in history and sociology. To illustrate the program for a history of sport as a history of modern bodies, another quotation might be of some help. The baseball historian Jules Tygiel, an expert on Jackie Robinson, the first African American to cross the color line of major league sport in the United States, once explained his motivation as such:

> As a fan, I focus primarily on what is happening on the field. As a historian, however, I am more interested in the broader cultural milieu that surrounds the game – how developments in the game of baseball reflect American society and the ways in which our nation has changed over time.[23]

Here, Tygiel describes the research design paradigmatic of the international sport historiography of the last two decades – a social history approach that is not interested primarily in results and records any longer but that tries to ask questions that relate sport activities to their social and cultural contexts. Nevertheless, Tygiel's self-reflexive explanation is not entirely satisfying. A history of sport as a history of modern bodies should take the body, its movements and the meanings attributed to them as the guiding axis for analysis. And in order to do just this, one should be very much interested in what is actually happening on the field, on the track, in the pool, in the gymnasium, or in the park. The movements of athletes' bodies in sport do actually mean something, which becomes clear in both the stories of Alick Wickham and Annette Kellerman. The "lad from the islands" that used a rotating arm stroke in combination with a parallel kick of both legs was helpful in sparking the imagination of a new nation, and the white woman from the end of the world made her swimming, diving, dancing and acting body an interdiscursive icon for the 'new woman' of the early twentieth century. Both stories circle around specific motion sequences, their performances, their acquirement and denomination, their analyzing, learning and training, their representations. A thick description, to use Clifford Geertz' phrase, of such movements in sport and physical culture can open new windows in analyzing modern power relations inscribed onto human bodies. But such a thick description has to be embedded into the contemporary discursive setting, in what Tygiel called the "broader cultural milieu that surrounds the game," in a fabric of meaning structured by intertextual and other references. From this point of view, the sportive bodies and their meanings in a complex web of cultural power relations become inseparable; it is their necessary contingency that makes sport and physical culture a suitable lens for cultural history.

IV.

As the examples of Wickham and Kellerman show, taking individual athletes and teams might be a suitable starting point for the project of a transnational history of sporting bodies in motion in the Pacific. They were on the move in the Pacific region somewhere between Australia and New Zealand, between the US West Coast, Hawai`i and other Pacific Islands – crossers of borders, benders of conventions and of standards. Their movements, voluntarily or forced, either with a clear destination or not, either linear or circular, alone or with others, created a certain spatial setting of routes and zones of contact, interaction, transfer, conflict at a time when their traveling was just one element in an increasing awareness of bodies in motion. The growing interest for sporting bodies became their cultural capital.[24] Those athletes became part of constituting modern concepts of the body. They were shaped by discourse as much as they were able to add to them new layers of meaning, to change and transgress them. Wickham and Kellerman were not unique; there are plenty of stories to tell about athletes traveling the Pacific. Think about Hawai`i's Duke Kahanamoku, who is considered the 'father of surf,' or about Dawn Fraser, the Australian Olympic swimming champion of the 1950s who had to undergo some hardships in order to verify her gender. Or think about Japanese athletes attending US colleges, something common in the interwar decades when political tensions between the US and imperial Japan caused hostilities. The 1904 St. Louis Olympics might serve as a final example: organized and held as some kind of sideshow of the parallel World Fair, it strongly combined ideas of the 'natural athlete' with modern conceptions of sport. The close proximity of Anthropology Days and Olympic Games underscore the role of modern sport for establishing racial hierarchies.[25]

But let us conclude this article with final thoughts on Alick Wickham and Annette Kellerman. The foundation myth of the 'Australian Crawl' as a cultural narrative tells a lot about the fascination around Wickham's origin from the Salomon Islands and what that notion of fascination meant for 'White Australia.' The imagination of the Pacific realm and its inhabitants was a constitutive element in a new nation's quest for collective identity and its multilayered power relations. Human beings from the close or distant islands were part of a complex web of race relations. There were some conflicting racial hierarchies discussed in contemporary Australia, but all of them idealized 'white,' Anglo-Saxons – *Caucasians* – at the top of the racial ladder and placed Aboriginals even below its lowest rung. *Islanders* – Papuans, Kanakas, Polynesians, Melanesians – were considered only slightly above them, and in the nineteenth century were needed and exploited labor migrants that could easily be expelled on the basis of several laws regulating the constitutive rule of whiteness in the becoming and then new nation.[26] But the Wickham story demonstrates that the racial discourse was far from stable and straightforward. Instead, it was highly ambiguous and contained important elements of exoticness and fascination, stimulated by the presence of traveling narratives and artifacts like postcards, pictures and films. So Alick Wickham, although a 'dusky lad,' could not only be perceived as a formidable, admired athlete, which might be interesting enough in itself, but he could also be 'whitened' and accepted as a 'true' Australian, even as founder of a valued national tradition. He serves as an example how bodily, biological, racialized attributes and stereotypes mark individual athletes and help explain their achievements – like it is nowadays still common sense that African Americans are born sprinters and long jumpers and people from Kenya are natural long distance runners.[27] And when – as in the case of Wickham – such naturalized attributes are combined with 'white' meticulousness and ideas of scientific progress, then the *tuppa ta pala* changes into the 'Australian Crawl.'

In that sense the Wickham story also reveals the gendered dimension of modern sport around 1900: as sport was mainly conducted by male athletes for male spectators, it established, stabilized and essentialized dominant versions of gender. With adapting a superior swimming style used by island inhabitants, some of their 'nimbleness' and body orientation could be integrated into the hegemonic conception of white masculinity. Moreover and at the same time, and this becomes clear when Annette Kellerman is also included in the picture, the expert discourses of medicine and biology were rearticulated in the authoritative voices of coaches that defined female bodies as deficient and declared sport and physical activity at best as not explicitly detrimental for female bodies' 'proper function,' namely biological reproduction.[28]

At least for middle class white women, the spirit of competition and seeking success in sport were commonly regarded as inappropriate, with the exception of golf, tennis, or swimming. Thus, Kellerman was able to use her ability to move – referring to different layers of meaning of that word – in order to cross boundaries, test possibilities and bend the limitations of gender conventions that proved to be less fixed and stable. Kellerman's case also indicates the role of media representations in charging the modern body with transnational meaning. They were not only an index for the 'value' of Annette Kellerman as commercial product, but also an influential part in establishing and charging the visual as *the* register for discussing gender in a fluent time and space.

There are even more aspects that link the stories of Wickham and Kellerman to ideas about sport history as a history of modern bodies. Enthusiasm for sport and competition are further key words. It is astonishing how long and densely something profane as a new, faster swimming style was debated at that time in public and in competing types of media. Much the same is true for the imaginative power aroused by a 'hot' newly designed and innovatively cut swim suit. Experts from different disciplines discussed and evaluated the crawl and became part of an ongoing accumulation of knowledge about bodies, its capabilities and limits in professional sport. *En passent*, but equally importantly, these discussions elaborated on national character and relations to neighbors in the Pacific, on different people living there. Both a motion sequence like the crawl and the embodied icon of Annette Kellerman were more or less official export products of the new Australian nation. They helped in elevating the political and cultural positions of Australia in the (South) Pacific and put Sydney onto the map as a city with successful school of swimmers.

Finally, it is illuminating to see how both the Wickham myth and the success story of the 'Mermaid of the Sea' made their way into the social memory of sport-crazy Australia and how they were retold again and again, eventually forming a linear narrative of success. In 1952, a film company made a documentary on Alick Wickham, entitled *Evolution of the Australian*

Crawl.[29] The production basically uses Hellmrich's book *How to Swim* as its script. It renarrates how the fastest way of swimming was invented in Sydney and how it conquered the world; it informs the viewers of Wickham's roots on the Solomon Islands, emphasizes his central role by establishing the new style, depicts the cheer of the coach and thus the baptizing, and recounts the following debates and experiments. Since then, the images of that movie from the 1950s reappeared in numerous sport documentaries, always showing a young Islander mimicking Alick Wickham, and one of them closing with the phrase: "We have taught the whole world how to swim."[30]

Notes:

1 Gary Osmond and Murray G. Phillips, "'The Bloke with a Stroke.' Alick Wickham, the 'Crawl' and Social Memory," The Journal of Pacific History 39,3 (2004): 309-24; eid., "'Look at that Kid Crawling' – Race, Myth and the Crawl Stroke," Australian Historical Studies 37,127 (2006): 43-62.

2 See i.e. the report on Wickham's first race in Sydney Sportsman, 13 Mar. 1901, 7.

3 Referee, 22 Jan. 1913, 4. The name *tuppa ta pala* appears in this article also, see 9.

4 Referee, 18 Mar. 1914, 11.

5 Dudley Hellmrich, How to Swim. A Comprehensive Booklet on Swimming, Surfing, and Natation Generally (Sydney: MacRae Knitting Mills, 1930).

6 Reet A. Howell and Maxwell L. Howell, A History of Australian Sport (Drummoyne, NSW: Shakespeare Head Press, 1987); John Bale, Landscapes of Modern Sport (Leicester: Leicester University Press, 1994).

7 Douglas Booth and Colin Tatz, One-Eyed. A View of Australian Sport (Sydney: Allen & Unwin, 2000), 72-88, 149-51; Dennis H. Phillips, Australian Women at the Olympic Games (Sydney: Walla Walla Press, 2001), 27-9; Emily Gibson (with Barbara Firth), The Original Million Dollar Mermaid. The Annette Kellerman Story (Sydney: Allen & Unwin, 2005).

8 Peter Catapano, "'The Perfect Woman.' Annette Kellerman and the Spectacle of the Female Form," Proteus. A Journal of Ideas 25,2 (2008): 23-7.

9 Dudley A. Sargent, "Modern Dances as Athletic Exercises," New York Times, 3 Jan. 1909, SM7. See also Patricia Vertinsky, The Eternally Wounded Woman. Women, Doctors, and Excercise in the Late 19th Century (Manchester/New York: Manchester University Press, 1990).

10 John Harley, "Sync or Swim? Plebiscitary Sport, Synchronized Voting, and the Shift from Mars to Venus," South Atlantic Quarterly 105,2 (2006): 409-28. See also Jennifer M. Bean, "Technologies of Early Stardom and the Extraordinary Body," Camera Oscura 16,3 (2001): 9-57, esp. 9-12.

[11] Katherine M. H. Blackford, Analyzing Character, the New Science of Judging Men. Misfits in Business, the Home and Social Life (New York: The Review of Reviews Company, 1916), 157-8.

[12] "Willst du jemanden ausprobieren – Dame oder Herrn – geh nicht ins Theater, auch nicht tanzen – geh auf Reisen, aber auf sportliche, fahre Ski mit dem auszuprobierenden Geschöpf, oder Auto am besten. Nichts decouvriert derart, nichts enthüllt den Charakter so sehr wie der Sport [...] Nur der Sport kann's zeigen." Erika Mann, "Sport und Charakter," in Tempo 1931, reprinted in Blitze überm Ozean. Aufsätze, Reden, Reportagen, eds. Irmela v. d. Lühe and Uwe Naumann (Reinbek bei Hamburg: Rowohlt, 2000), 92-3. It is interesting how negatively Mann refers to dancing – which without any doubt played a prominent role in conceptualizing and living the modern body in motion.

[13] For a general view see Phillip Prodger, Time Stands Still. Muybridge and the Instantaneous Photography Movement (New York: Oxford University Press, 2003); Tom Gunning, "Movies, Stories, Attractions," in American Cinema, 1890-1909. Themes and Variations, ed. André Gaudreault (New Brunswick, NJ: Rutgers University Press, 2009), 112-32.

[14] Ralph J. Poole, "Männer im Pelz. Entblößungen und Verhüllungen des natürlichen Körpers um 1900," in Väter, Soldaten, Liebhaber. Männer und Männlichkeiten in der Geschichte Nordamerikas. Ein Reader, eds. Jürgen Martschukat and Olaf Stieglitz (Bielefeld: transcript, 2007), 159-82.

[15] In general see Allen Guttmann, From Ritual to Record. The Nature of Modern Sport (New York: Columbia University Press, 2004 [1978]).

[16] "Sportberichterstattung [darf] keineswegs als bloße diskursive Verdoppelung eines 'eigentlichen Sports' verstanden werden." Felix Axster, Jens Jäger, Kai Marcel Sicks and Markus Stauff, "Einleitung. Mediensport als Praxis der Grenzziehung," in Mediensport. Strategien der Grenzziehung, eds. eid. (München: Wilhelm Fink, 2009), 7-20, 7.

[17] Stated in an unpublished manuscript "Writing the History of Sport" (1991), see Jeffrey Hill, "British Sports History. A Post-Modern Future?" Journal of Sport History 23,1 (1996): 1-19, 2.

[18] Patricia Vertinsky, "Time Gentlemen Please. The Space and Place of Gender in Sport History," in Deconstructing Sport History, ed. Murray G. Phillips (Albany: State University of New York Press, 2006), 227-45, 234-5.

[19] Andreas Eckert, "Sport und Kolonialismus in Afrika," Geschichte in Wissenschaft und Unterricht 56,10 (2005): 565-79; John Bale and Mike Cronin, eds., Sport and Postcolonialism (Oxford/New York: Berg, 2003).

[20] Uta Andrea Balbier, "'Spiel ohne Grenzen'. Zu Stand und Perspektiven der deutschen Sportgeschichtsforschung," Archiv für Sozialgeschichte 45 (2005): 585-98.

[21] Editorial "Sport," WerkstattGeschichte 15,44 (2006): 3-4.

[22] For a survey see Matthias Marschik, Rudolf Müller, Otto Penz and Georg Spitaler, eds., Sport Studies (Wien: Facultas, 2009).

[23] Jules Tygiel, Extra Bases. Reflections on Jackie Robinson, Race, and Baseball History (Lincoln, NE: University of Nebraska Press, 2002), xi.
[24] Philip A. Mosely, Richard Cashman, John O'Hara and Hilary Weatherburn, eds., Sporting Immigrants. Sport and Ethnicity in Australia (Sydney: Walla Walla Press, 1997); Andrew Honey, "Sport, Immigration Restriction and Race. The Operation of the White Australia Policy," in Sport, Federation, Nation, eds. Richard Cashman, John O'Hara and Andrew Honey (Sydney: Walla Walla Press, 2001), 29-42.
[25] John Bale, "From Anthropology Days to the Anthropological Olympics," in The 1904 Anthropology Days and Olympic Games. Sport, Race, and Imperialism, ed. Susan Brownell (Lincoln, NE: University of Nebraska Press, 2008), 324-42. See also James Gilbert, Whose Fair? Experience, Memory, and the History of the Great St. Louis Exposition (Chicago: University of Chicago Press, 2009).
[26] Andrew Markus, Australian Race Relations, 1788-1993 (Sydney: Allen & Unwin, 1994), 12; Raymond Evans, Kay Saunders and Kathryn Cronin, Race Relations in Colonial Queensland. A History of Exclusion, Exploitation, and Extermination (St Lucia: University of Queensland Press, 1993).
[27] Kevin Hylton, 'Race' and Sport. Critical Race Theory (New York: Routledge, 2009); John M. Hoberman, Darwin's Athletes. How Sport Has Damaged Black America and Preserved the Myth of Race (New York: Houghton Mifflin, 1997); John Bale and Joe Sang, Kenyan Running. Movement Culture, Geography and Global Change (London: Frank Case, 1996).
[28] Vertinsky, "Time Gentlemen Please" and Roberta J. Park, "A Decade of the Body. Researching and Writing About the History of Health, Fitness, Exercise and Sport, 1983-1993," Journal of Sport History 21,1 (1994): 59-82.
[29] Evolution of the Australian Crawl; 1952, produced by Kingcroft Australia.
[30] 90 Years of Australian Swimming; 1999, produced by the Australian Swimming Association.

White Subjects, Governmentality, and Immigration Restriction in the United States, 1894-1924

Robert Júlio Decker

I. Introduction

Over the course of the last fifteen years, whiteness studies have evolved from a field of political activism into a diverse and complex academic formation. Nowadays, the notion that whiteness and other racial classifications are constructed and thus can be historicized and contextualized with the categories of gender and class has spread to various academic fields. Far from being a monolithic discipline, it is a tool, an analytic backdrop against which a number of topics are investigated.[1]

Whiteness studies' nature as both a political project and an analytical tool blurs the boundaries between political agency and historical or sociological analysis. Moreover, the application of whiteness studies in sociology, history, and political science in the so-called third wave is one of the factors contributing to the diversity of approaches, but also to the lack of a coherent use of its terms and a uniform theoretical background.[2] Whiteness has thus been repeatedly criticized for its "arbitrary and inconsistent definitions" and its "conceptual imprecision."[3]

One of these shortcomings is the indiscriminate use of the concept of power. Power is mentioned in almost every attempt to describe the elusive and altering character of whiteness: as a way to guarantee privileged access to economic, political or social resources; as a way to perpetuate a dominant position in the cultural production of racial formations; or as a social construct which is reflected in juridical-political frameworks. While these different interpretations do not necessarily contradict each other, a more fruitful way to integrate power into the conceptual framework might be the employment of Michel Foucault's theories, as some researchers have suggested.[4] Whiteness scholars mostly concentrate on the idea of power as a white economic and political privilege, which is assumed to have been formed over centuries and to still be unconsciously or consciously perpetuated by individuals. Therefore, the deconstruction of whiteness is supposed to raise awareness of this privilege and to empower subjects to overcome the underlying structure of racial discrimination. According to Ladelle McWorther, the logical flaw in this interpretation of power is the presupposition of an independent subject instead of one prefigured by racially defined relationships and networks of power. While whiteness scholars postulate the ideal of a subject that recognizes and overcomes the limitations imposed by racial constructs, they tend to neglect the influence of these constructs in the very creation and recreation of the subjects themselves.[5]

In Foucault's later work, he interpreted power not as a mode of subjugation, as being limited to law or disciplining institutions, but insisted on analyzing it in its local and unstable "multiplicity of force relations."[6] By investigating power in terms of the set of mechanisms and procedures which are integrated into all social relations and in a perspective that traces power from below, "at its outer limits where it becomes capillary [...] the place where it implants itself and produces its real effects" can be located.[7] According to Foucault, modern Western societies increasingly augment the older models of sovereignty and discipline, which exerted power through laws, punishment or corporeal techniques, by governmental management. Governmentality does not exclusively focus on single subjects, but aims at the population as a whole and draws on the subjects' willingness for self-regulation and for improving society.[8] The subjects thus become nodal points where different technologies of power intertwine; they are constituted by power relations.[9] Applied to whiteness studies, it can be argued that power does not only establish technologies of self-discipline and self-conduct, but also constitutes the subject as a "racial self," to quote Ann Laura Stoler.[10] Thereby, it can be explained why subjects do not only participate in processes of racial othering, but also perceive themselves as white and help to extend and optimize the apparatus of the racial state.

This article will demonstrate how whiteness studies can benefit from Foucault's theoretical framework by applying it to the discourses on immigration restriction in the Unites States between 1894 and 1924. Re-examining a topic many whiteness scholars have already dwelled on from a new perspective may clarify the role of subjects in the promulgation of whiteness.[11] Therefore, this article will first follow the traditional line in whiteness studies by tracing the edification of a narrower definition of whiteness limited to Anglo-Saxons in the biopolitical knowledge of the population (II.). It will then analyze the roles of individuals and groups in transferring these concepts into public and political discourses before they were eventually condensed into a palpable apparatus of security (III.).

II. Biopolitics and the Production of Whiteness

From the mid-1970s, Foucault shifted his analytical focus from disciplinary techniques to the more complex and broader technologies of power. In his concept of governmentality, biopower/biopolitics (Foucault uses these terms interchangeably) become crucial measures to enable the modern state to exert more control over the population. In contrast to older forms of power, which exerted the right "to *take* life or *let* live," biopower is a productive power which introduces a new right: the power "to 'make' live and 'let' die."[12] Apart from the corporeal subjugation of individuals through discipline and training, biopower includes forms of "*regulatory controls: a bio-politics of the population*."[13] It calculates with regularities of deviance and compliance to maximize the population's productive and desired aspects. To identify deviant subjects, an "inflation of forms and bodies of knowledge, of discourse, a multiplication of authorities and decision-making elements" occurs.[14] In this context, state racism reintroduces death into the nexus of power. Foucault states that the idea of race is utilized "to create caesuras within the biological continuum addressed by biopower." He describes its compelling internal logic as follows:

> The more inferior species die out, the more abnormal individuals are eliminated, the fewer degenerates there will be in the species as a whole, and the more I – as species rather than individual – can live, the stronger I will be, the more vigorous I will be.[15]

Foucault emphasizes that "death" or "elimination" in this regard do not only imply physical destruction, but also have to be understood as every form of "indirect murder:" by "increasing the risk of death for some people, or, quite simply, political death, expulsion, rejection."[16]

Governmentality no longer merely establishes strict rules and punishes individuals who break them, but installs "security mechanisms [...] around the random element inherent in a population of living beings so as to optimize a state of life."[17] These apparatuses of security or *dispositifs* comprise discursive as well as non-discursive elements, connecting series of knowledge to discursive formations, institutions, laws, practices and technologies to manage the internal and external threats to society.[18]

Both of biopower's elements – to enhance desired tendencies within the population and to defend it from perceived threats – require new series of knowledge to function within the governmental setting. The population has to be constructed as "a datum which depends on a set of variables," a "set of elements in which we can note constants and regularities" to be constituted as an object amenable to governmental management.[19] This observation relates to Foucault's notion that power and knowledge are intrinsically entangled and constitute one another.[20] In the second half of the nineteenth century, two different series of knowledge gained in importance: statistics and the social sciences.

In the United States, the largest set of data was provided by the American census. By creating the population in its normality, the census made it feasible, calculable, predictable and thereby "at least partially susceptible to rational management."[21] Under Francis A. Walker, superintendent of the census from 1870 to 1889, renowned social scientist and leading political economist, the census gradually evolved into "a full-fledged instrument to monitor the overall status of American society."[22] The vastly increasing amount of data combined statistics for administrative needs, vital statistics and so-called "moral statistics." The data was organized by multiple "grids of specification;" the most important was race, following the censal "tradition of [racial] differentiating."[23] By formalizing racial differentiations in a "process of objectified nomination," the census "has worked thus to draw racial lines around and within the society, reifying as it reflects prevailing racialized common sense," to quote

David Theo Goldberg.[24] In the second half of the nineteenth century, these differentiations became more refined. In 1870, census collectors began to distinguish between native and foreign-born inhabitants and those "of foreign parentage."[25] As Matthew Hannah has pointed out, immigrants were thereby constructed as a "statistical race" with significant implications – all subcategories of the census could thus be tabulated by these 'new races.'[26] Hence, the census did not only constitute the population in its normality, making it accessible to governmental management, but also differentiated the normal extent of deviance along racial lines.

This new demographic and statistical data enabled multiple interpretations by the increasingly specialized disciplines within the academe. The normal occurrence of deviance could be calculated by using statistical data which allowed the perception, analysis and prediction of general trends and principles of the population.[27] The emerging academic fields of medicine, anthropology, psychiatry, and criminology provided explanatory models and means to classify deviant behavior to identify the groups Foucault defines as "those who deviate from that norm, [...] those who pose a threat to the biological heritage."[28] New rationalities of scientific knowledge established a "binary rift" within society between the normal and the obverse, the latter representing the exception to the rule it defined.[29] These new forms of power/knowledge transformed social and political conflicts into technical problems, recasting them "in the neutral language of science."[30] White male scientific experts represented the professionalization and specialization in the sciences and became authorities on social problems in public and political discourse, helping to detect the 'true' nature of a problem and then finding and implementing a solution.[31] This allowed for obviating the nature of biopolitical measures: they were no longer perceived as "the representation of power as law" or the direct exertion of power, but appeared to be a series of necessary and justified state interventions, a biological imperative on behalf of the population's security to maximize and protect life.[32]

This historical development within the sciences coincided with fundamental changes in the discourses on immigration and on the essence of whiteness. Several scholars have pointed out that whiteness in this context functioned as a central organizer in American political life and was repeatedly reclassified.[33] Different immigrant groups were repeatedly depicted as distinct and inferior races, which put into question their ability to become part of American society. While German and Irish immigrants eventually were regarded as white in the late nineteenth century, Chinese and Japanese immigrants were excluded in 1882 and 1907, respectively, because of their supposed racial difference.[34] In the last quarter of the nineteenth century, the racialization of immigrants was broadened, now encompassing the so-called new immigrants from Eastern, Southeastern and Southern Europe. Drawing on the tradition of scientific racism in biology and anthropology, new scientific discourses in genetics, evolutionary theory and the social sciences redrew the boundaries of whiteness and expanded existing racial hierarchies. Even prior to the rediscovery of Mendel's laws of inheritance, scientists became convinced that Europe was populated by various distinct races. William Z. Ripley subsumed earlier findings in 1899 when he distinguished between the "superior Teuton race" and the gradually inferior "Alpine and Mediterranean races."[35] Thus the distinctions between Asian, African-American, Native American and the white race were not only perpetrated, but the white race became itself increasingly fragmented, leading to a "variegated whiteness," as Jacobson has pointed out.[36] Adhering to the logic of whiteness to define itself by racial othering, this process depicted the new immigrants as being not fully white, as "inbetween peoples" in the racial hierarchy, above African-Americans and Asians, but distinctively below the "Nordic race."[37]

In 1888, Richmond Mayo-Smith, a pioneer in the field of political economy, introduced the distinction between old immigrants and so-called new immigrants, comparing the latter to African-Americans: "they certainly possess the value of the slave, who was also ignorant, unskilled and often degraded."[38] In his opinion, only the "defective and delinquent classes, who are only a burden" were coming to the United States by that time, a fact he undergirded by referring to census data about the higher proportion of new immigrants among criminals, paupers and inmates of mental institutions.[39] In the discussion of the qualities of the incoming immigrants, Mayo-Smith combined the discourses on differences between multiple European 'sub-races' and on deviance within the American population, applying statistical data to underline his argument. Apart from his work for the census, Francis A. Walker emphasized the new immigrants' 'racial inferiority' in many of his writings, pleading for a rigid regiment of restriction. In an 1896 article for the *Atlantic Monthly* he emphasized the racial dangers of immigration to the United States:

> [the new immigrants] have no history behind them which is of a nature to give encouragement. They have none of the inherited instincts and tendencies which made it comparatively easy to deal with the immigration of the olden time. They are beaten men from beaten races; representing the worst failures in the struggle for existence. Centuries are against them, as centuries were on the side of those who formerly came to us. They have none of the ideas and aptitudes which fit men to take up readily and easily the problem of self-care and self-government, such as belong to those who are descended from the tribes that met under the oak-trees of old Germany to make laws and choose chieftains.[40]

In his writings, Walker thus classified new immigrants as a separate, non-white race, simultaneously defining the Anglo-Saxon 'racial qualities' by describing the lack of these in the *racial other*. Moreover, he delineated the qualities he deemed to be inherently characteristic for the Anglo-Saxon male, namely the ability to govern oneself and others to become a worthy and integral part of the American body politic.

Walker and Mayo-Smith are only two examples of a general trend within the sciences towards a narrower definition of the 'white superior race' confined to an assumed common Northern European origin.[41] This new conception of an "absolute whiteness," as Matthew Pratt Guterl characterizes it, supports Jacobson's statement that the "racial sciences were in fact racializing sciences" and led to the facilitation of scientific proof of the new immigrants' 'inherent racial inferiority.'[42] After the turn of the century, the rediscovery of Mendelian genetics and the subsequent rise of eugenics in the United States added to the intensification of the discourse about white racial qualities, concentrating on genetic reasons for 'white superiority,' deviance within the 'Nordic' or 'Aryan' race and the dangers of 'racial miscegenation' through immigration. Contemporary authors such as Madison Grant, John R. Commons or Charles B. Davenport not only popularized the knowledge of the assumed racial threat of immigration, but discussed the 'superior qualities' of the 'Teuton' race at considerable length in numerous successful books and articles.[43]

This contravenes the consensus within whiteness studies that whiteness itself is an "unmarked marker," unnamed, empty or invisible, at least to white people themselves, but indicates that white racial qualities in this period were the subject of elaborate scientific investigations and intensified public discourses.[44] Although whiteness studies have scrutinized the history of racial discourses in the United States at length, this issue has hardly been problematized.[45] One of the few exceptions is Julian Carter, who has argued that the equation of whiteness with normality was a process that occurred between the 1890s and the 1930s. In order to determine the essence of whiteness, not only its boundaries, but its actual characteristics were discussed in detail, which is reflected by the enormous amount of sources explicitly dealing with 'Nordic' or Anglo-Saxon racial characteristics.[46]

To summarize, biopower established an extensive knowledge of the American population to divide it into the 'normal' and the 'deviant' and to defend the 'normal' population from the latter. This was accomplished by the increasingly complex technologies of the census, which incorporated notions of scientific racism to decode data on deviance by race. This data was interpreted by the emerging social sciences to distinguish between the old, desirable immigration and the new immigrants who were classified as undesirable due to supposedly higher rates of deviance. Combined with discourses on the racial superiority of whites, citizens felt the need to urge the state to restrict immigration to protect the racial essence of whiteness.

III. Governmentality, Progressivism, and the White Subject

As argued above, the discursive formations of these 'racial dangers' first emerged in the sciences and utilized statistical data about normality and deviance within the population. Towards the end of the nineteenth century, these formations began to traverse from the scientific into the public and political discourse, with a growing demand for state action to establish apparatuses of security around the field of immigration. In order to localize and situate the concrete steps in this process, we have to return to Foucault's notions of governmentality and subject formation.

In contrast to older forms of power, the governmental citizen no longer is the mere object of power, but at the same time the subject of its agency within the limits set by discourse and governmental actions.[47] This new citizen-subject thus is not only subjugated by coercion and domination if necessary, but also incorporates technologies of the self.[48] This new form of power is applied in the liberal society as "the management of freedom," it releases the subjects' self-interests and desires in such a way that they serve the common weal.[49] The introduction of the social as a sphere simultaneously connects the subject to the state and confuses the boundaries of responsibility between the two. Civil society becomes "the interface [...] of governors and the governed."[50] The amalgamation of the public and the private opens new areas to governance, which rules through indirect power, through "the conduct of conduct. [To] govern, in this sense, is to structure the possible field of action of others."[51] Alongside the objectification of the subjects as elements of the population in governmental knowledge, the subjects are constituted "as a 'fold-back' [...] of the governmental mode of power."[52] Individuals are not entirely subjected, but interiorize techniques of surveillance and discipline as "techniques" or "practices of the self" and thereby contribute to "the auto-production of security."[53]

If this approach is combined with whiteness as an analytical concept, it can be argued that in this particular period, white male subjects were not only constituted as self-regulating and responsible citizens, but in many cases also as white or Anglo-Saxon Americans. Therefore, the productive dimension of power/knowledge also constituted "racial selves."[54] These new governmental subjects considered the protection of the 'American race' to be their civic duty and disseminated scientific findings about assumed racial dangers to the public and political discourses, thereby contributing to the constitution of other racialized citizen-subjects.

One important institution in this process was the *Immigration Restriction League* (IRL). Founded in 1894 in Boston by Harvard alumni, the League became one of the first modern political lobbies in the United States. Comprising of influential men from politics, science and education, its "membership rolls did read like a *Who's Who* of American education and civic leadership."[55] The aforementioned Ripley, Mayo-Smith and Walker as well as men such as John Fiske, Nathaniel Shaler, Madison Grant, John R. Commons, Owen Wister, A. Lawrence Lowell, Edward A. Ross, David Starr Jordan and Henry Holt became members or vice-presidents of the League. The IRL never exceeded 900 members; most of the workload was managed by founding members Robert DeCourcy Ward and Prescott F. Hall.[56] After the Spanish-American War, they could rely on the financial support of Boston philanthropist Joseph Lee and were able to employ Joseph H. Patten for lobbying activities in Washington.[57] The League distinguished itself from earlier and contemporaneous nativist and anti-Catholic movements by underscoring their reliance on scientific findings. In its constitution, the League emphasized that their commitment was "non-sectarian and non-partisan" and stated that its goal was

> to arouse public opinion to the necessity of a further exclusion of elements undesirable for citizenship or injurious to our national character. It is not an objective of this League to advocate the exclusion of laborers or other immigrants of such character and standards as fit them to become citizens.[58]

In order to distinguish 'desirable' from 'undesirable' immigrants, the IRL followed a scientific approach in investigating the problems of immigration, compiling their own statistics from census data and obtaining additional data from state and private institutions, including charities, mental institutions, and chambers of commerce. Additionally, IRL representatives intermittently visited Ellis Island to investigate illiteracy rates. They even convinced immigration officers to use the League's preferred methods of tabulation to differentiate literacy rates by national origin.[59]

In an age when the American society incrementally became industrialized and urbanized, the IRL depicted the new immigrants as a threat to free labor and the stability of the political system. The League ascribed modern society's problems to immigration by providing 'scientific evidence' of the new immigrants' assumed racial inferiority. It linked them to crime, poverty, low standards of living and sanitation, and mental and physical defects. In frequently published pamphlets with titles such as "Study these Figures and Draw your own Conclusion," the IRL provided statistical data comparing rates of criminality, insanity and pauperism in relation to the immigrants' proportion of the whole population. Using census data to distinguish between total numbers, native whites and foreign-born, the pamphlets emphasized that in 1890, for example,

> 41.56 per cent of white inmate population in the almshouses of the U.S. is native white [while] 58.44 per cent is of foreign element. [...] Thus a foreign population which is 17 per cent of the total white population, furnishes nearly 1-2 [half] of the white paupers in the U.S.[60]

These figures were published annually by the IRL, whose publications came to include more detailed statistics, thereby constituting statistical evidence and predicting rising crime rates and social unrest if immigration would not be restricted. As their preferred measure of regulation, the IRL championed a literacy test, primarily because the members believed in its power to exclude immigrants of an ostensibly detrimental racial kind. In a pamphlet published in 1895, the League emphasized the racial otherness of the latest immigrants:

> The immigration of the last few years has brought us hundreds of thousands of aliens, from various countries of Europe, who are foreign not only in race, language and customs, but in habits of thought, traditions, and ways of living. Until within a few years our immigration was almost entirely made up from the best peoples of Europe, peoples akin to us in language or in origin, of one race with ourselves, and capable of ready and rapid assimilation. Lately, however, this has changed. [...] [Now] the most ignorant, the most undesirable and the least capable of assimilation [are coming].

The authors therefore pleaded for the literacy test:

> It will debar a considerable proportion of the least desirable immigrants [...]. The educational test is a moderate, rational, effective and simple means of further restricting immigration to this country.[61]

These scientific and statistical 'facts' were disseminated by the League in numerous newspaper articles and editorials, talks and publications and added to the creation of public awareness of the 'problems' of immigration. In transferring these findings to public and political discourse, the League resembled other progressive era reform movements. Their typical pattern contained the identification of a social problem, the formation of an association, scientific investigation of the problem, the creation of public attentiveness, the generation of remedies, and eventually their implementation by government agencies. Despite their diverse political goals and varying memberships in the specific organizations, reform movements of the progressive era can be summarized in their shared attempt to create a "new people living by new codes of conduct" by combining "applied reason and active citizenship."[62] Progressives' struggles were an attempt to improve other individuals and to turn them into responsible citizens zealous to combine their efforts for the common weal.

In order to preserve the purpotedly superior white qualities, IRL members considered it their personal obligation as citizens to protect the US from assumed racial deterioration through immigration. Interpreted in Foucault's concept of biopolitics, the IRL thus used these systems of knowledge to pledge for "taking control of life and the biological processes of man-as-species."[63] In constructing racial difference, the League ascribed social deviance to the new immigrants and championed restriction as a biological necessity, thereby acting on behalf of the state to preserve social and racial stability.

Although the League had been founded before the rise of the eugenic movement, IRL leaders soon recognized the similarities between their own and the eugenicists' arguments and even considered renaming their organization *Eugenic Immigration League*.[64] While the eugenic movement first concentrated on so-called degenerates *within* the Anglo-Saxon population, trying to prove that they were "not quite white" (to use Matt Wray's term), the IRL soon began to cooperate with eugenicists and tried to convince them of the importance of immigration restriction.[65] In the League's opinion, racial improvement could be achieved not only by enhancing the desired traits of the domestic white population, but the influx of so-called inferior race stock from abroad had to be stopped as well. Thus, IRL executives were in close contact with eugenic institutions and their most prominent leaders, namely Madison Grant, Charles B. Davenport and Lothrop Stoddard.[66] In 1904, six years before the most important eugenic research institute in the United States, the *Eugenics Record Office*, was founded, Prescott Hall published an article on "The Selection of Immigration." In this article, Hall pointed out that immigration

> is *the* most important problem of our time, and, as such, deserves the careful study of our citizens. We are the trustees of our civilization and institutions with a duty to the future, and as trustees the stocks of population in which we invest should be limited by the principle of a careful selection of immigrants.[67]

Hall therefore appealed to other citizens to also become aware of their responsibilities as members of the white race to engage in politics and to urge more rigid restrictions. He argued that it was not sufficient to talk "of regulating marriage with a view to the elimination of those unfit *for other purposes than mere survival*" but appealed to readers to realize "that here in the United States we have a unique opportunity, through the power to regulate immigration, of exercising artificial selection upon an enormous scale." Immigration regulation should therefore be used to admit "races [...] not kindred in habits, institutions and traditions" only in small quantities.[68]

This description of the eugenic interpretation of immigration by no means intends to construct a single monolithic conception of whiteness or to deny the "messiness of race."[69] To use Howard Winant's words, "variable, conflictual, and contested [...] *racial projects*" coexisted in this particular period in the United States, all backed by their own scientific findings and strains in public discourse.[70] The concepts of Americanization, the melting pot, cultural pluralism, and Anglo-Saxon supremacy with their accompanying political implications all vied for public approval.[71]

The League was not the only or most important institution within the process of the new immigrants' racialization, however, it did play a significant role as a nodal point between scientific and public discourses and their political implementation. The IRL propagated a redefined concept of whiteness that linked racial superiority to the preservation of the American nation. Based on their own self-perception as normal and responsible citizens, IRL members were persuaded that they had to take action on behalf of the state. They therefore were convinced that "to point out wherein our immigration laws need strengthening for the better protection and preservation of the race is a duty," as Prescott F. Hall expressed his views.[72] To urge other citizen-subjects to actively engage in this affair was part of this duty, as well.

The creation of the *Dillingham Commission* in 1907, which investigated the so-called immigration problem for three years, provided an opportunity for the IRL to submit its own views on the subject. In 1910 and 1911, the IRL posted two slightly differing sets of questionnaires to a list of individuals comprised from a copy of *Who's Who in America*. The selection of recipients reflected the IRL executives' gendered conception of political and social relevance, exclusively addressing men, including lawyers, clergymen, educators and doctors.[73] In these letters, the League asked which method of immigration restriction the recipients preferred. Providing statistics, the letter pointed out that existing immigration laws were

> inadequate to preserve the present physical, mental and moral status of our people, to say nothing of eugenic improvement; and that the policy of admitting those who have or will have defective children means a weakening of the nation and a needless and heavy increase in public and private burdens.[74]

The IRL sent 3800 questionnaires to the names from *Who's Who*, receiving 375 replies favoring and 28 opposed to any further restriction. Another 3381 letters were sent to graduates of the Harvard medical school leading to 157 replies with only one disagreeing with further restriction.[75] The rate of return seems to be rather low and suggests that only those who already were concerned about racial and eugenic issues might have answered. Nonetheless, these replies can be used as a small sample for higher middle class educated men and at least indicate that many of the recipients had already developed a consciousness of their racial selves and the importance of guarding their 'Anglo-Saxon superiority' from the assumed threats of immigration. One C. W. Abbot, Jr., replied that

> I am convinced after much study and thought on the subject, that the time has come when most drastic measures are absolutely necessary to prevent great harm to the future of our country. [...] [O]ur very existence is seriously threatened by the presence already of millions of people whom I believe we can never properly assimilate. I would therefore stop all immigration now.[76]

James Franklin Ailshie, justice of the Iowa Supreme Court stated that

> I cannot see how anyone who is at all familiar with conditions as they now exist and who knows of the thousands of immigrants who are

> flocking to our shores every month and the great percentage of crime and illiteracy they represent would not be in favor of much more rigid restrictions and regulations on the subject of immigration. It seems to me that we ought to inquire into their ancestry and previous conduct and conditions more fully than we do at present.[77]

Furthermore, many statements can be found that illustrate the respondents' awareness of their racial status in relation to the new immigrants and their concern for the biological essence of the population. The attorney Charles O. Bailey highlighted that

> the immigration question should be considered from a racial instead of an educational or financial point of view. I would favor the exclusion of immigrants belonging to other than the Aryan races and would place severe restrictions upon any excepting the western nations of Europe. It is physically impossible for races ethnologically distinct to become assimilated into a homogeneous mass. The United States was originally settled by the races of Western Europe and belongs to them.[78]

Others referred to the new immigrants as a "constant introduction of low-grade material into our social structure which has a steadily weakening and deteriorating effect" or mentioned that they "have no Saxon tradition or training; they are non-assimilable under our institutions, and they bring with them and establish here new crimes."[79] According to the prevailing scientific theories of the time, criminality was also regarded to be a racial characteristic, which could be passed on to future generations, as the reply of one S. Whiney exemplifies:

> The important thing is obviously to keep out all persons who are either individually or racially criminally inclined, or lacking in capacity for development, and to encourage the coming here of those, whether they may be poor or not, who themselves, or through their progeny, promise to make good citizens, and, in the end, contribute to the moral, intellectual and physical improvement of the country.[80]

The respondents also referred to their specific local racial encodings. John Norton Pomeroy from the Pacific Coast praised Chinese exclusion as an example of successful regulation: "We frankly admit, and always have admitted, that our fundamental objection to the immigration we wish to exclude is *racial*."[81] Inhabitants of the Southern states frequently related the issue of immigration to African Americans, stating that "we do not need statistics to show the injurious effect of pauper immigrants upon our people – even our Negroes are injured by contact with them."[82] One respondent from Virginia gave a more detailed account of his reflections on this question, emphasizing the citizen's responsibility to protect the American population:

> In my judgment, the greatest mistake that this, or any other, country ever made, was the importation of negroes; and hundreds of years will doubtless elapse before the many questions arising out of the presence of that unfortunate race in this country have been settled.
> While there are doubtless races in Europe or Asia as unassimilable with our race as the negroes are, yet, in many cases, it is only a difference in degree, and unless some check is put upon the unrestricted outpouring upon us of these individual degenerates and members of unassimilable races, I believe posterity will rise up to curse us for our folly or neglect.[83]

Many of the respondents promised to write to their Senators and Congressmen to urge them to enact legislation to regulate and limit immigration. The IRL's actions thus not only contributed to the construction of racial selves, but also helped to transform subjects into active citizens by directly appealing to their racial self-perception and their responsibility for the future of the American nation and race. The League had laid the foundation for the discursive connection of immigration and eugenic improvement by raising the subjects' awareness of their personal responsibility. In response to the IRL's questionnaire, Charles B. Bancroft, physician at the New Hampshire State Hospital in Concord, wrote:

> The actual setting of any scheme of eugenic improvement is of course surrounded with immense difficulty. One method of attaining such improvement must be the result of a careful inspection of imigrants [sic] that are pouring into this country from foreign lands. It seems to me that if we can only establish a high standard of intelligence in the people that enter the country we have made one big stride toward the attainment of at least the beginning of eugenic improvement.[84]

Eventually, a selection of these replies to the questionnaires was handed over to the *Dillingham Commission*. In its preliminary remarks to the questionnaire responses, the IRL emphasized that restriction was necessary not only from the economic, social and moral standpoint, but also for eugenic reasons:

> The same arguments which induce us to segregate criminals and feeble-minded and thus prevent their breeding apply to excluding from our borders individuals whose multiplying here is likely to lower the average of our people. We should exercise at least as much care in admitting human beings as we exercise in relation to animals or insect pests or disease germs.[85]

The commission finally published its findings in 1911 in 41 volumes, including a *Dictionary of Races and People*. Underpinning racial hierarchies with extensive data, the commission recommended the introduction of the literacy test "as the most feasible single means of restricting undesirable immigration."[86]

The IRL kept on lobbying for restriction by using their numerous different approaches to establish a connection between immigrants' 'racial inferiority' and deviant behavior. Esteemed as scientific experts, IRL members repeatedly advised Congressional committees on the question of immigration restriction. Attempts to pass the literacy test regularly either failed in Congress or were vetoed by Presidents who believed in the American tradition of unrestricted European immigration. Congress had already failed to overcome the presidential veto in 1897, similar bills were again vetoed in 1912 and 1915; eventually Congress overruled President Wilson's second veto in 1917.[87]

With the end of First World War and the rise of the *Red Scare*, the political climate was ripe to end the American tradition of unrestricted European immigration. In 1921, the *Immigration Act* was passed. It limited the number of immigrants to three per cent of each European nationality living in the US, this number being determined by the census of 1910. This national quota system was revised in 1924 by an *Immigration Commission* presided over by Congressman Albert Johnson, who had been in close contact with restrictionists and eugenicists for years. He assigned Harry Laughlin, superintend of the *Eugenic Records Office*, as an "expert eugenics agent," who provided the commission with extensive statistical data about the new immigrants' deviant characteristics.[88] The eugenic and the restrictionists' logics complemented one another in their shared aim to protect the racial essence of whiteness. In 1924, Congress passed the *Reed-Johnson Act* after a debate which had been dominated by biological and racial arguments. The act reduced national origin quotas to two percent and shifted their basis to the census of 1890, thereby significantly reducing the number of the new immigrants.[89] This system, although slightly changed in 1929, stayed in effect until the 1960s, reducing the overall number of immigrants as well as assuring that most of them came from Northwestern Europe.

The history of the IRL presents us with an example of how whiteness was reconfigured between the 1890s and the 1920s. The findings of scientific racism and eugenics and the production of statistical knowledge limited the category of whiteness to Anglo-Saxonness. The League transferred this narrower definition to public discourse through statistics, questionnaires and various publications. It formalized the racial boundaries and contributed to the racial othering of the new immigrants. On the other hand, the League associated the 'Anglo-Saxon racial essence' with social stability and the progress of the nation. No longer an "unmarked marker," whiteness became both a powerful impetus and means to intervene in the political process. Acting voluntarily to protect the nation from an assumed racial deterioration, the League exerted pressure on politicians to reform immigration legislation – an influence that would affect the composition of the US population for decades.

More significantly, however, the IRL's history can also serve to more fully communicate the intricate entanglements of whiteness, power and racialized subjects. IRL members reached out to individuals to make them agents of the biopolitical project of the protection of population and state. Calling on the special duty of each and every member of the 'superior Anglo-Saxon race,' the League interpolated subjects simultaneously as citizens and racial selves. Using other white subjects' awareness of their racial status, the IRL encouraged them to call for the enactment of a state apparatus of security and regulation. In a Foucauldian sense, this governmental process meant that the state no longer had to impose regulations, but merely implemented and codified its citizens' suggestions to protect the essence of whiteness.

Notes:

---

[1] An early version of this paper was presented at the *Australian Critical Race and Whiteness Studies Association Conference* in Melbourne in December 2008. I would like to thank the participants for the helpful feedback. Furthermore, I would like to express my gratitude for comments on this article and for general support to Kate Dossett, Simon Hall, Matt Wray, and Say Burgin.

[2] France W. Twine and Charles Gallagher, "The Future of Whiteness. A Map of the 'Third Wave'," Ethnic and Racial Studies 31,1 (2008): 4-24.

[3] Eric Arnesen, "Whiteness and Historians' Imagination," International Labor and Working-Class History 60 (2001): 3-32, 5, 23.

[4] Ladelle McWorther, "Where do White People Come From? A Foucauldian Critique of Whiteness Studies," Philosophy & Social Criticism 31,5-6 (2005): 533-56; Aileen Moreton-Robinson, "Towards a New Research Agenda? Foucault, Whiteness and Indigenous Sovereignty," Journal of Sociology 4 (2006): 383-95; George Yancy, "A Foucauldian (Genealogical) Reading of Whiteness. The Production of the Black Body/Self and the Racial Deformation of Pecola Breedlove in Toni Morrison's The Bluest Eye," in What White Looks Like. African-American Philosophers on the Whiteness Question, ed. George Yancy (New York: Routledge, 2004), 107-42.

[5] McWorther, "Where Do White People Come From," 543-7.

[6] Michel Foucault, An Introduction. The History of Sexuality Vol. 1 (New York: Vintage, 1990), 93-4.

[7] Michel Foucault, Society Must Be Defended. Lectures at the Collège de France, 1975-1976 (New York: Picador, 2003), 27-8.

[8] Michel Foucault, Security, Territory, Population. Lectures at the Collège de France, 1977-1978 (Houndmills: Palgrave Macmillan, 2007), 107-10.

[9] Foucault, Society Must Be Defended, 28.

[10] Ann Laura Stoler, Race and the Education of Desire. Foucault's History of Sexuality and the Colonial Order of Things (Durham: Duke University Press, 1995), 95.
[11] See for example Theodore W. Allen, The Invention of the White Race (London: Verso, 1995); Noel Ignatiev, How the Irish Became White (New York: Routledge, 1995); Matthew Frye Jacobson, Whiteness of a Different Color. European Immigrants and the Alchemy of Race (Cambridge, Mass: Harvard University Press, 1998); David R. Roediger, Working Toward Whiteness. How America's Immigrants Became White. The Strange Journey from Ellis Island to the Suburbs (New York: Basic Books, 2005).
[12] Foucault, An Introduction, 136; id., Society Must Be Defended, 241.
[13] Foucault, An Introduction, 139. Original emphasis.
[14] Michel Foucault, The Birth of Biopolitics. Lectures at the Collège de France, 1978-1979 (Basingstoke: Palgrave Macmillan, 2008), 250.
[15] Foucault, Society Must Be Defended, 255.
[16] Ibid., 256.
[17] Ibid., 246.
[18] Michel Foucault, "The Confession of the Flesh. A Conversation with Alain Grosrichard, Gerard Wajeman, Jacques-Alain Miller, Guy Le Gaufey, Dominique Celas, Gerard Miller, Catherine Millot, Jocelyne Livi and Judith Miller," in Power/Knowledge. Selected Interviews and Other Writings, 1972-1977, ed. Colin Gordon (Harlow: Pearson Education, 1980), 194-228, 194-5.
[19] Foucault, Security, Territory, Population, 71, 74.
[20] Michel Foucault, Discipline and Punish. The Birth of the Prison (Harmondsworth: Penguin, 1979), 27; Michel Foucault, Politics, Philosophy, Culture. Interviews and Other Writings, 1977-1984, ed. Lawrence D. Kritzman (New York: Routledge, 1988), 106.
[21] Matthew G. Hannah, Governmentality and the Mastery of Territory in Late Nineteenth Century America (Cambridge: Cambridge University Press, 2000), 25.
[22] Margo J. Anderson, The American Census. A Social History (New Haven: Yale University Press, 1988), 85.
[23] Michel Foucault, The Archeology of Knowledge (London: Tavistock, 1972), 42; Hannah, Governmentality, 30, 56-9; Anderson, The American Census, 12.
[24] David T. Goldberg, Racial Subjects. Writing on Race in America (New York: Routledge, 1997), 33-4.
[25] Sharon M. Lee, "Racial Classifications in the US Census, 1890-1990," Ethnic and Racial Studies 16,1 (1993): 75-94, 76.
[26] Hannah, Governmentality, 143, 209.
[27] Mary Poovey, A History of the Modern Fact. Problems of Knowledge in the Sciences of Wealth and Society (Chicago: University of Chicago Press, 1998), 26-31.
[28] Foucault, Society Must Be Defended, 61.

---

29 Ibid.
30 Hubert L. Dreyfus and Paul Rabinow, Michel Foucault. Beyond Structuralism and Hermeneutics. With an Afterword by and an Interview with Michel Foucault (Chicago: University of Chicago Press, 1983), 196.
31 Hannah, Governmentality, 72; Robert F. Zeidel, Immigrants, Progressives, and Exclusion Politics. The Dillingham Commission, 1900-1927 (DeKalb: Northern Illinois University Press, 2004), 3.
32 Dreyfus and Rabinow, Michel Foucault, 185.
33 Allen, The Invention of the White Race; Ignatiev, How the Irish Became White; Jacobson, Whiteness of a Different Color; Roediger, Working Towards Whiteness.
34 Ibid. For Asian immigration see Erika Lee, At America's Gates. Chinese Immigration during the Exclusion Era, 1882-1943 (Chapel Hill: University of North Carolina Press, 2003); Bill O. Hing, Making and Remaking Asian America through Immigration Policy, 1850-1990 (Stanford: Stanford University Press, 1995).
35 William Z. Ripley, The Races of Europe. A Sociological Study (New York: Johnson Reprint, 1965 [1899]).
36 Jacobson, Whiteness of a Different Color, 41.
37 James R. Barrett and David R. Roediger, "Inbetween Peoples. Race, Nationality and the 'New Immigrant' Working Class," Journal of American Ethnic History 16,3 (1997): 3-44.
38 Richmond Mayo-Smith, "Control of Immigration II. Do We Need the Immigrants?" Political Science Quarterly 3,2 (1888): 197-225, 211.
39 Richmond Mayo-Smith, Emigration and Immigration. A Study in Social Science (New York: Johnson Reprint, 1968 [1890]), 178.
40 Francis A. Walker, "Restriction of Immigration," in Discussions in Economics and Statistics, ed. Francis A. Walker (New York: A. M. Kelley, 1971), 437-51, 447.
41 For this trend see for example Robert J. C. Young, The Idea of English Ethnicity (Malden: Blackwell, 2008).
42 Matthew Pratt Guterl, The Color of Race in America, 1900-1940 (Cambridge, Mass.: Harvard University Press, 2001), 27-51; Jacobson, Whiteness of a Different Color, 33.
43 John R. Commons, Races and Immigrants in America (New York: Kelley, 1967); Charles B. Davenport, Heredity in Relation to Eugenics (New York: Holt, 1911); Madison Grant, The Passing of the Great Race. Or, the Racial Basis of European History (New York: Scribner, 1916).
44 Birgit Brander Rasmussen, Eric Klinenberg, Irene J. Nexica, and Matt Wray, "Introduction," in The Making and Unmaking of Whiteness, eds. Birgit Brander Rasmussen, Eric Klinenberg, Irene J. Nexica, and Matt Wray (Durham: Duke University Press, 2001), 1-24; Ruth Frankenberg, "The Mirage of an Unmarked Whiteness," in ibid., 72-96.

[45] For first attempts see Robert M. Vanderbeck, “Vermont and the Imaginative Geographies of American Whiteness,” Annals of the Association of American Geographers 96,3 (2006): 641-59, 643, 648; Eva Bischoff, “Between Animal Instinct and Morality. The Construction of White Masculinity in Medico-Psychiatric Discourse in Weimar Germany,” in Historicising Whiteness. Transnational Perspectives on the Construction of an Identity, eds. Leigh Boucher, Jane Carey and Katherine Ellinghaus (Melbourne: RMIT Publishing, 2007), 427-35.

[46] Julian B. Carter, The Heart of Whiteness. Normal Sexuality and Race in America, 1880-1940 (Durham: Duke University Press, 2007), 1-41.

[47] Barbara Cruikshank, The Will to Empower. Democratic Citizens and Other Subjects (Ithaca: Cornell University Press, 1999), 19-23.

[48] Michel Foucault, The Use of Pleasure (New York: Vintage, 1990), 10-1; Graham Burchell, “Liberal Government and Techniques of the Self,” in Foucault and Political Reason. Liberalism, Neo-Liberalism and Rationalities of Government, eds. Andrew Barry, Thomas Osborne and Nikolas Rose (Chicago: University of Chicago Press, 1996), 19-36; Mitchell Dean, Governmentality. Power and Rule in Modern Society (London: Sage, 1999), 10-6; Nikolas Rose, Powers of Freedom. Reframing Political Thought (Cambridge: Cambridge University Press, 1999), 40-7.

[49] Foucault, The Birth of Biopolitics, 63; Foucault, Security, Territory, Population, 72-79.

[50] Gilles Deleuze, Foucault (London: Continuum, 2006); Cruikshank, The Will to Empower, 6; Foucault, The Birth of Biopolitics, 297.

[51] Colin Gordon, “Governmental Rationality. An Introduction,” in The Foucault Effect. Studies in Governmentality. With Two Lectures by and an Interview with Michel Foucault, eds. Graham Burchell, Colin Gordon and Peter Miller (London: Harvester Wheatsheaf, 1991), 1-48, 2. Although this term never appeared in one of the official translations of Foucault’s work, the use of Gordon’s own translation of “conduire des conduits” is nonetheless widespread; Dreyfus and Rabinow, Michel Foucault. Beyond Structuralism and Hermeneutics, 221.

[52] Sebastian Harrer, “The Theme of Subjectivity in Foucault’s Lecture Series L’Herméneutique du Sujet,” Foucault Studies 2 (2005): 75-96, 83.

[53] Foucault, The Use of Pleasure, 26-30; Goldberg, The Racial State, 104.

[54] Goldberg, The Racial State, 104; Stoler, Race and the Education of Desire, 95.

[55] Matthew Frye Jacobson, Barbarian Virtues. The United States Encounters Foreign Peoples at Home and Abroad, 1876-1917 (New York: Hill and Wang, 2000), 197.

[56] For general information on the IRL see Barbara Miller Solomon, Ancestors and Immigrants. A Changing New England Tradition (Cambridge, Mass.: Harvard University Press, 1989); for details of the IRL’s involvement in the politi-

cal process see Daniel J. Tichenor, Dividing Lines. The Politics of Immigration Control in America (Princeton: Princeton University Press, 2002); Zeidel, Immigrants, Progressives, and Exclusion Politics.

[57] Immigration Restriction League (US) Records, bMS Am 2245, fMS (1051), Houghton Library, Harvard University.

[58] Immigration Restriction League, Constitution, 1894, IRL Scrapbooks, Vol. I: Jul. 12 1894 – May 29 1895.

[59] Immigration Restriction League, Annual Report of the Executive Committee for 1896, IRL Scrapbooks, Vol. VI: Jan. 1 1897 – Apr. 26 1897.

[60] Immigration Restriction League, Study These Figures and Draw Your Own Conclusions, Publications of the Immigration Restriction League, no. 2 (1894), Widener Harvard Depository, US 10583.9.

[61] Immigration Restriction League, The Educational Test as a Means of Further Restricting Immigration, Publications of the IRL, no. 6 (1895).

[62] Michael E. McGerr, A Fierce Discontent. The Rise and Fall of the Progressive Movement in America, 1870-1920 (New York: Free Press, 2003), 79; Leon Fink, Progressive Intellectuals and the Dilemmas of Democratic Commitment (Cambridge, Mass.: Harvard University Press, 1997), 13.

[63] Foucault, Society Must Be Defended, 246-7.

[64] IRL Records, Minutes of the Meetings of the Executive Committee (Vol. 3), 14 Dec. 1911, IRL Records, MS (1052).

[65] Matt Wray, Not Quite White. White Trash and the Boundaries of Whiteness (Durham: Duke University Press, 2006), 65-96.

[66] IRL Records, bMS Am 2245 (342, 468, 469); Joseph Lee Papers, Massachusetts Historical Society, I, A, Carton 1. Stoddard even became a member of the IRL's executive committee in the early 1920s.

[67] Prescott F. Hall, "Selection of Immigration," Annals of the American Academy of the Political and Social Sciences 24,1(1904): 169-84, 184.

[68] Ibid., 170-1.

[69] Roediger, Working Towards Whiteness, 37.

[70] Howard Winant, Racial Conditions. Politics, Theory, Comparisons (Minneapolis: University of Minnesota Press, 1994), 24.

[71] Desmond S. King, Making Americans. Immigration, Race, and the Origins of the Diverse Democracy (Cambridge, Mass.: Harvard University Press, 2000), 14-36.

[72] Prescott F. Hall, Second Report of the Committee on Immigration of the Eugenics Section of the American Genetics Association, 1914, IRL Records, bMS Am 2245 (1065), folder 1.

[73] United States Immigration Commission, Statements and Recommendations Submitted by Societies and Organizations Interested in the Subject of Immigration, Reports of the Immigration Commission 41 (Washington, D.C.: Government Printing Office, 1911), 110.

[74] IRL Records, Series I, B, Circular letters: 1908-1914, MS Am 2245 (1047).

[75] US Immigration Commission, Statements and Recommendations Submitted, 110-11. IRL Records, Minutes of the Meetings (Vol. III), 1 Jan. 1910, 25 Mar. 1910, 11 Apr. 1910, 19 Apr. 1911, 31 Oct. 1911, 2 Nov. 1911, MS (1052).
[76] IRL Records, bMS Am 2245 (6).
[77] IRL Records, bMS Am 2245 (15).
[78] IRL Records, bMS Am 2245 (75).
[79] IRL Records, bMS Am 2245 (118, 584).
[80] IRL Records, bMS Am 2245 (977).
[81] IRL Records, bMS Am 2245, (769), original emphasis.
[82] IRL Records, bMS Am 2245, (364).
[83] IRL Records, bMS Am 2245, (171).
[84] IRL Records, bMS Am 2245 (88).
[85] US Immigration Commission, Statements and Recommendations, 106-7.
[86] US Immigration Commission, Abstracts of Reports of the Immigration Commission: With Conclusions and Recommendations and Views of the Minority (In Two Volumes: Vol. I), Reports of the Immigration Commission 1 (Washington, D.C.: Government Printing Office, 1911), 48. For the Dillingham Commission see Zeidel, Immigrants, Progressives, and Exclusion Politics.
[87] Tichenor, Dividing Lines, 138-41.
[88] Ibid., 143-6.
[89] Mae M. Ngai, "The Architecture of Race in American Immigration Law. A Reexamination of the Immigration Act of 1924," Journal of American History 86,1 (1999): 67-92.

Sovereignty, Identity, and Indigeneity: The Case of Hawai`i

Judith Schachter

I. Introduction

In the summer of 2004, I met the King of Hawai`i at the home of Auntie Eleanor. We were having lunch when two young Hawaiian men walked in. Auntie Eleanor set two more plates – there was enough food to feed any stranger who might wander in. Talk over lunch was desultory and slow – I learned not to talk "business" while eating, though I was curious about the two men. Gradually the conversation shifted to the business at hand, and lasted for five hours without a pause.

The gist was Victor's claim that the "throne" continued to exist, that the American take-over had been "illegal," and that he was the rightful inheritor of the crown.[1] To claim sovereignty, he said, was "ridiculous," since the Hawaiian people never relinquished their sovereign nation state and the Hawaiian kingdom had consequently never vanished. He carried notebooks of genealogy, which he showed to Auntie Eleanor. He needed her authority, and her testimony to the legitimacy of his claims to be king. She was a respected and wise elder – a *kupuna* – in the community.

Together we looked at pages of genealogy and Auntie Eleanor validated Victor's ancestry. She thereby emphasized a key concept in individual appropriations of identity and of status: tracing connections back through past generations. Genealogy places an individual in a social network, providing a criterion for membership in a collectivity that may be the *`ohana* (family) or *kalahui* (the nation). Inasmuch as an individual cites ancestry in order to claim affiliation, the process overrides biological connection. Moreover, citations of ancestry are supplemented by behavior – appropriate actions – opening the door to incorporation even further. This lends Hawaiian notions of belonging the expansive inclusiveness characteristic of Polynesian cultures.[2] On the ground, this means that most 'Hawaiian' families contain individuals with, for instance, *haole*, Asian, or Tongan backgrounds.[3] Hawaiian understandings of belonging are far from the ascribed ethnic and racial rules of inclusion and exclusion brought by the *haole* and institutionalized under US colonial law and practice. *Identification* of the island's residents by American governing authorities contends with the *identities* individuals construct through genealogical reckoning and demonstrated traits.

Eleanor studied Victor's genealogy and listened to the words he used in stating his claim. Satisfied with both the documentation and his purpose, at the end of the afternoon, she advised him to argue his case "strongly." "You cannot stand in the shadow of the *kūpuna*," she told him, sending him on his way.

Her message, seemingly straightforward, embeds several points. Eleanor sent Victor on his way as a member of the cohort to whom she bequeathed the burden (*luhi*) of directing the future of Hawai`i. Her parting words assert the role of the *kūpuna* and the limits of that role. Carriers of wisdom, the *kūpuna* transmit values of the past to the present and inculcate ways of being Hawaiian in a younger generation. But to act in a political arena, as Victor intended and as Eleanor wisely perceived, requires different strategies and calculations. In claiming the throne, Victor claimed both a form of sovereignty and a model for membership in a nation. For Hawaiian kingdom activists anybody who can demonstrate that their ancestors were subjects of the king – whether native or *haole* – is still a member of the Hawaiian nation.[4] And for Victor the nation state had only to be reaffirmed. He consequently dismissed the US as audience for his petition and looked instead to an international arena (he asked me about UN documents).[5] An illegal, occupying force, the US did not merit his attention.

From an outsider's perspective the resurrection of the Hawaiian kingdom is not a politically realistic idea. For the vocal groups of Hawaiian kingdom activists, it is a powerful and attractive idea that allows the imagining of a restored Hawaiian nation. The idea erases the colonial past without confronting its impact on the islands and its inhabitants.

The Hawaiian kingdom activists represent only one, and not the most influential position in the diverse movement for Hawaiian sovereignty. The afternoon with Victor, however, exemplifies the deeper social basis of a political debate about Hawaiian self-determination which at first glance seems to resonate primarily with a small group of political activists: adherents of the Hawaiian kingdom, Hawaiian nationalists, or proponents of a Native Hawaiian government set up by the US Congress. At second glance, an immersion in daily conversations and in recurring media commentary reveals the spread of the debate, and the different directions the arguments take. Yet a common theme runs through the diverse approaches: discussions of sovereignty in twenty-first century Hawai`i hold an assessment of US imperialism and constitute an unusually forthright critique of a colonial presence that remains in force today. American legal, social, and political systems structure the life of every resident of the islands.

When the subject of sovereignty comes up, individuals at the proverbial kitchen table, in the media, and at public forums offer a history of the relation between Hawai`i and the United States. While details and viewpoints vary, the fact of an illegal take-over of one nation by another remains constant. No less constant are references to the consequences of this take-over in the imposition of foreign categories for classifying and administering a population. *Haole* dominance accentuates the problem of who identifies as Native Hawaiian and who has the power to legitimize the identity of Native Hawaiian. Even spelling reflects administrative intrusion: Native with a capital "N" refers to persons of Hawaiian ancestry; native with a lower case "n" refers to people with 50% or more Hawaiian blood. I come back to the point later.

Resolving the problem involves parsing out the meanings of genealogy, nationality, and identity, and these meanings are entangled in the encounter between colonizer and colonized. In the end, I argue in this article, none of the resolutions escape the race-making that is colonialism's most devastating ideology.

II. Fieldwork

I have been doing fieldwork in Hawai`i since 1989. I did not start with an interest in sovereignty but with an inquiry into the role of kinship for preserving Hawaiian cultural identity in an American state. During the 1990s questions the sovereignty movement raised about self-determination and self-governance increasingly dominated conversations I had with the people I had come to know, on O`ahu and on the Big Island.[6] The encounter with Victor was only one, though in some ways the most striking incidence of talk about sovereignty I experienced. It became impossible to ignore the repercussions of this debate in the recent two decades of my fieldwork.

Eleanor is the sister of John, the *kupuna* who welcomed me into his family, his *`ohana*, soon after my arrival in Hawai`i. He took on the task of transforming my status from *malihini*, or stranger, to *kama`āina*, the child of the land I could become by learning Hawaiian culture. John spent his life negotiating Hawaiian and American identities, and he applied the personal experience of "beach crossing" to his collaboration in my project.[7] His view of being Hawaiian shaped his assessment of the sovereignty movement, and influences my account. I draw on the voices of John and Eleanor because they shared stories with me, granting me insight into the subtle and complex responses of two Hawaiian elders to a movement led by actors who operate predominantly in the political arena.[8]

John did not live to see the *Native Hawaiian Government Reorganization Bill* introduced by Senator Daniel Akaka in 2000 and still pending in Congress – although the House passed the Bill in mid-February 2010.[9] Eleanor did know of the Senator's proposal. The document, called the *Akaka Bill* or sometimes *Akaka*, proposes a process for establishing a Native Hawaiian government. Reprinted in newspapers and on the Internet, the Bill is accessible to every individual in the State of Hawai`i, along with its several amendments. Its impact is clear in the controversies dividing political activists and pervading debates at kitchen tables, on beaches, and in the shopping malls of the islands. The *Akaka Bill* frames my discussion of sovereignty, identity, and indigeneity in Hawai`i for three reasons.

First, the *Akaka Bill* places that discussion in the context of US imperialism and control over the archipelago. The Bill aims at – or "provides" as the author of the Bill hopes – "a structured process of reconciliation for both Native Hawaiians and non-Native Hawaiians to finally address and resolve longstanding issues resulting from Hawaii's painful past."[10] Arguments about the fate of Hawai`i inevitably refer to the United States, regardless of position or person. In public conversations and in private settings, individuals who discuss the issue end up probing the impact of American law and assessing the survival of Hawaiian culture through two centuries of conquest.

Second, the Bill spells out the scope and limits of self-determination that the US government (in the best of circumstances) is willing to grant to a "Native Hawaiian governing entity." In doing so, the Bill offers interpretations of *indigenous* that implicate Native Americans, Alaskan natives, and Native Hawaiians. Moreover, the language of the Bill demonstrates the complexities of separating the concept of indigenous from the notion of race.

Third, whatever the legal competences and material resources of the envisioned organization, definite criteria must be established for designating the subjects (or members, in *Akaka's* term) of the "Hawaiian governing entity." Establishing such criteria, however, is not a simple administrative act of identifying those citizens who, in the eyes of the US government, are entitled to be part of a "Native Hawaiian membership organization." Behind the debate over criteria lies the residue of imperial intervention: who has the power to define Hawaiian, how, and for what purposes? The answer, never singular, goes way beyond the decision of individuals to identify themselves as native or indigenous, as members of a Native Hawaiian 'nation' or 'community.' The definition governs the distribution of resources, the granting of Homestead leases, and the terms of entry into the state's educational, economic, and political institutions.

Changes in the American legal system and shifts in political regimes in Hawai`i over the last century have not altered the paradigm for defining the Native Hawaiian. The definitions and concepts of identity applied by authorities are inexorably shaped by colonial race-making strategies. More importantly, these strategies shape the way the US responds to demands for indigenous rights, sovereignty, and self-determination. In their efforts to start a process of reconciliation, the proponents of the *Akaka Bill* clearly try to get away from these race-making strategies. However, they cannot – I will argue in the following sections – escape the legacy of the colonial categorization of indigenous people in the United States.

III. Native Hawaiians as "a Dying Race"

Mainland Americans tend to see the inhabitants of the Hawaiian Islands through a distinct looking glass. References to race characterize every public discussion of Hawai`i-US relations, from the time of missionary arrival to President Clinton's 1993 *Apology*. *Akaka* is not an exception.

In the late nineteenth century, Congressmen openly referred to race in arguing for or against the incorporation of Hawai`i into the United States. Easing the conscience of reluctant colonizers, legislators portrayed Hawai`i as the recipient of benign American rule and a potential site of racial harmony. US presence civilized the natives and fended off the "yellow peril." Opponents of Territorial status maintained that the racial composition of Hawai`i posed a threat to the United States as an Anglo-Saxon nation. Useful as the archipelago might be economically, the opponents continued, its incorporation as a domestic entity would demolish the political and cultural institutions of the United States.[11]

Ultimately, in 1898, proponents of annexation won. The victory was the culmination of a century-long conquest of the islands that extended the 'manifest destiny' expansionist policy of the United States into the Pacific. In 1893, a small cadre of American forces had deposed the last reigning monarch of the Hawaiian nation. Five years later, in the Spanish-American war of 1898, the US completed its expansion from California to China with the acquisition of the Philippines and Guam.[12] In 1900, Congress passed the *Organic Act* which incorporated Hawai`i into the United States. From then on, the Territory of Hawai`i was fully subject to American laws.

As important as the extension of the American rule of law over the islands was for the Hawaiians, it obviously served one political purpose: What runs like a thread through the dozens of hearings in Congress on the status of Hawai`i between 1880 and the 1950s is the search for policies that ensure the rule of a minority of white settlers over indigenous Hawaiians and Asian immigrants.[13]

The Hawaiian population did not create an obstacle in the US government's path to ensuring American supremacy. Already discussions about the annexation of Hawai`i had taken for granted that "the decadence and extinction of the native race" was inevitable – as the Secretary of State, James G. Blaine, put it in 1881. The absolute menace to the United States, which Blaine and his allies wanted to fend off with the annexation of Hawai`i, was the "replacement by another [race], to which the powers of Government would necessarily descend."[14] If the United States does not try to Americanize Hawai`i through incorporation, Blaine's widely shared argument went, power would fall to the rapidly growing number of Asian "coolie workers" the white plantation owners had brought in.[15]

The effort to stop the influx of Asian workers and to exclude resident Asians from the political and social rights of citizens gave rise to an array of racial policies. These included the *Gentlemen's Agreement* of 1907 that prohibited Japanese contract workers from moving to the US mainland, a racially based housing policy on the plantations, the gradual elimination of Japanese language schools, and the *Oriental Exclusion Act* of 1924 which was finally repealed in 1952.[16]

In this context, Native Hawaiians were perceived as a placid minority deserving of special benefits and protection in return for their political support of the *kama`āina-haole* elite.[17] Acknowledging the precarious living conditions of the Native Hawaiians in the Territory, in 1921 the US Congress passed the

Hawaiian Homes Commission Act (HHCA) designed to rescue the "dying Hawaiian race" by returning "the people" to the land.[18] Proposed by Prince Jonah Kalaniana`ole Kūhi`ō, Territorial representative to Washington and a favorite of the deposed Queen Lili'uokalani, the Act allotted land to Native Hawaiians. Eighty years before Daniel Akaka introduced his Bill, also designed to "save" the Hawaiian people, the HHCA set terms that still permeate the Senator's proposal.

Like Akaka today, Prince Kūhi`ō faced Congress for several years, tailoring a Bill to the demands of House and Senate, the political elite in Hawai`i, and to the needs of his constituents – the Hawaiian people with whom he identified. In the end, the central proposal appealed to Congress and the Hawaiian oligarchs: placing people on the land resonated to a Hawaiian past and to an American construct of benign imperial rule.

For over a century, colonial authorities had preached the benefits of farming for civilizing and disciplining a recalcitrant population. Most significantly, the Bill won the support of the plantation owners in the Territory, whose interests – and domination of the Territory's economy – forced the Prince to a compromise. The HHCA left plantation land (thus the best acreage) in the hands of planters, with the stipulation that taxes from the land be used to support infrastructure on the Homelands. As a result, rehabilitation is distinguished from profitable agriculture in the substance of the Act.[19]

Prince Kūhi`ō and John Wise, the co-sponsor and missionary descendant, aimed at a "repatriation" of the land through its return to the people, the *kanaka maoli*. The category was broad, and the Bill specified first no and then a very low blood quantum restriction. Pressures to restrict the recipients further led Kūhi`ō and Wise to agree to provisions based on welfare and charity, in which "need" was redefined "in racial terms by using blood quantum as an indicator of social competency, where those defined by the 50-percent rule were deemed incapable of looking out for themselves."[20] The others, the many Native Hawaiians with 30% or 20% or 10% blood, were declared fit to compete in "mainstream" society. At the same time Native Hawaiians regardless of their blood quantum were looked upon as a pre-modern indigenous group that had to be forced to assimilate in order to overcome social and economic disadvantages in a rapidly Americanizing territory.

Claimants for land granted by the HHCA (Homesteads) had to prove blood quantum with official documents. Today the *Department of Hawaiian Home Lands* (DHHL), created in 1960 by the State of Hawai`i, administers the *Homestead Act* and decides on the submitted proof. In 1978, a Constitutional Convention in Hawai`i established the *Office of Hawaiian Affairs* (OHA) to distribute to Native Hawaiians the revenue from leased Hawaiian lands.[21] Like the DHHL, OHA uses a blood quantum to determine acceptable beneficiaries. In the bureaucratic parlance of the two agencies those who have the required 50% blood quantum are "native Hawaiian," while those with a lower blood quantum are labeled as "Hawaiian." The term 'Native Hawaiian' comprises both groups.[22]

The racialization of indigenous Hawaiians had a predictable outcome: the number of those who could claim to be "pure" Hawaiian diminished even further. As a result Native Hawaiians were still seen by many *haole* as vanishing – through intermarriage, assimilation, and migration to the mainland. The 'race' seemed to be dying.

But those labeled as dying never stopped identifying as Native Hawaiian. The legal and administrative categorizations inscribed in HHCA did not dismantle the terms of self-identification. To the surprise of many *haole*, Hawaiians with less than half Hawaiian blood defied their bureaucratic status as mixed or part and identified as Hawaiians. "The paradox was striking," Lawrence Fuchs stated in 1961. "As Hawaiians mixed with the rest of the community, they often maintained their feeling of 'Hawaiian-ness' [...] and the feeling of 'Hawaiian-ness' was intensified in many cases even though its character changed."[23] In the same year that Hawai`i became the fiftieth state, with a promise to every citizen of equal rights and opportunities, acute observers already noticed a "psychological rebirth of the Hawaiian people."[24] In the sixties, after a long period of forced acculturation and suppression of the Hawaiian language and culture, a Hawaiian renaissance swept the state. Diverse groups of Native Hawaiians started to reclaim cultural autonomy and indigenous rights.[25] Hawaiian immersion schools came into being in the 1980s, instituting Hawaiian as the language of instruction.

By 1990, emphasis on culture gave way to a movement for political change. OHA and DHHL became primary targets in the arguments for revising the North American role in Hawaiian affairs. Leaders and local *hui* (associations) joined in protest, claiming that governmental agencies discriminated against the people they were designed to serve. Protestors faulted the agencies for implementing a hegemonic definition of Native Hawaiian identity, resonant of a colonial history. In the rhetoric of protest, the concept of blood quantum perpetuates the racism in colonial policies.[26]

IV. Redefining the Status of Native Hawaiians: From Race to Tribe to Distinct Native Community

In 1993, President Bill Clinton apologized for the illegal take-over of a nation one hundred years earlier.[27] His statement prompted the senior senator from Hawai`i, Daniel Akaka, to draft the Bill he brought to Congress seven years later. The Bill proposes a new relationship between Hawai`i and the United States "by establishing a process within the framework of Federal law for the Native Hawaiian people to exercise their inherent rights as a distinct, aboriginal, indigenous, native community to reorganize a Native Hawaiian governing body for the purpose of giving expression to their rights as native people to self-determination and self-governance."[28]

Three crucial decisions hide behind this terse legal language, decisions that became a matter of heated debate in the following years.

To establish "the process within the framework of Federal law" means first that *Akaka* reconfirms the plenary powers of Congress which can in cases of overriding national interest repeal whatever authority to self-government the Federal Government may grant Native Hawaiians.[29] Secondly, the Bill assumes that Native Hawaiian self-government can be based on the nation within a nation relationship granted to American Indian tribes. Thirdly, *Akaka* implies that Native Hawaiians as a "distinct [...] community" represent a collective, political entity similar to Indian nations or tribes, retaining "some elements of quasi-sovereign authority, even after cession of their lands to the United States."[30]

The framework the Federal government used for the American Indians – the nation within a nation model – is premised on tribal political organization, and the assumption that the tribe determines membership in the nation. The model is based on the 1934 *Indian Reorganization Act*, which granted officially-recognized Indian tribes authority over local affairs and implemented the consolidation of individual land allotments into tribal hands. These reservation lands are held in trust by the *Bureau of Indian Affairs*, under the Department of Interior, and self-governance is limited by the plenary powers of the US Congress. Whether on reservation lands or not, American Indians can claim both US citizenship and tribal membership; criteria for tribal membership varies from tribe to tribe. Determinations of tribal identity are a subject of conflict: tribes may establish criteria that are not accepted by the Federal Government or vice versa. Moreover, the spread of DNA testing returns some tribes to biological calculations, despite the colonial legacy of such proof of identity.

The history of Native Hawaiians differs in many respects from Native Americans: they never had a tribal organization and they established a sovereign modern nation state only in the nineteenth century, in response to the threat of colonization. Yet in supporting self-governance for the Native Hawaiians, proponents turn to the *Indian Reorganization Act* as the most effective way of granting autonomy under the constitutional framework of the United States. At the same time, referring to the difference between Indian tribes and the Native Hawaiian community, some legal scholars and members of Congress conclude that the Native Hawaiians do not have any constitutional basis for their claim of self-determination. In contrast to tribes – they argue – membership in the Hawaiian community is indeterminate.[31]

For those who assume that indigenous Hawaiians have the same right to govern themselves as Indian tribes or Alaska Natives the different history and social organization of indigenous Hawaiians throws open the question of what makes "Native Hawaiians [...] a unique and distinct, aboriginal, indigenous, native people."[32] Who is, who can legitimately claim to be a Native Hawaiian, and who can make binding decisions about who will be included or excluded?

Deliberately avoiding the term nation, the *Akaka Bill* constitutes Native Hawaiians as a distinct people that governed itself in the past. In view of the obvious problem that the Native Hawaiians today lack a political entity that can legitimately claim to act on behalf of the Hawaiian people, the Bill resorts to an administrative reconstruction of a Native Hawaiian people and its government entity. This involves, first, appointing a commission (under the supervision of the US Secretary of Interior) that will set up a roll that contains all constituents who fulfill the membership criteria laid out in the Bill. The so-determined electorate then will ratify the governing documents in a referendum and finally establish the envisioned Hawaiian governing body.

However, without the prior definition of a membership roll, an administrative surrogate for a constituent assembly, the envisioned process of reorganizing a "Native Hawaiian Government entity" cannot start. According to Section 71 of the original Bill "the roll shall include the names of the adult members of the Native Hawaiian community who wish to become members of a Native Hawaiian governing body and who are the lineal descendants of the aboriginal, indigenous, native people who resided in the islands that now comprise the State of Hawaii on January 1, 1893, and who occupied and exercised sovereignty in the Hawaiian archipelago."[33]

With this definition Akaka endeavors to distance himself from the racial criteria of the Hawaiian Homestead law as well as the biological/essentialist implications of tribal identity. At the same time, the Bill leaves the question of who will qualify as a Native Hawaiian constituent wide open. In the first version of the Bill, Akaka offered a non-conclusive list of ways to prove Hawaiian descent (genealogical records, affidavits of *kūpuna*, church or census records). In the next version of 2001 the Bill added an alternative way to verify membership: eligibility in the programs authorized by the *Hawaiian Homes Commission Act*.[34] Reworked and amended by the legal experts in the Department of Justice the regulations on membership cover several pages in the 2009 version.[35]

Neither tribe nor Western-style nation state, the Hawaiian native community remains 'imagined' in *Akaka*, an assemblage of bureaucratic constructed constituents.[36]

Aiming at a "reconciliation process" between the US and Native Hawaiians, the *Akaka Bill* has had – for the moment at least – the opposite effect: fierce political and legal attacks from different directions. While vocal American opponents argue that Congress disregards the interests of the citizens of the state of Hawai`i in recognizing the special interests of a dubious Native Hawaiian community, activists of the sovereignty movement fear a repeat of the horse-trading that in 1921 left Hawaiians with a decisive blood quantum rule and some, often arid, land that was of no use to the plantation owners. For them the *Homestead Act* primarily helped the white oligarchy expand its grip on Hawaiian land.

As much as Akaka tried to avoid it, it is still race, the significance of racial policies and arguments in the colonial history of Hawai`i that emerges in the current debate in a twisted way. If race-making played a crucial role in marginalizing Native Hawaiians as a dying people in the twenties, race is now used to denounce Native Hawaiians as a group segregating itself in an alleged color blind society.[37] What drifts eerily through the current debate is the accusation that the call for collective rights is a call for the preferential treatment of the 'Hawaiian race,' threatening the equal rights of all American citizens.[38]

Inextricably intertwined with the racial argument is still the same question: What happened and should happen to the 1.2 million acres of land ceded in 1900 to the US government and still under her control? The *Akaka Bill* sidesteps this question and offers – through a newly established government entity – "an opportunity for Native Hawaiians to negotiate with the state and Federal Government to resolve longstanding legal issues," most of them over the ceded land.[39] The Bill, in other words, transforms the unsolved question of Hawaiian land into a procedural one between the Federal government, the State of Hawai`i, and the new Hawaiian government entity.

V. Creating a Hawaiian Race anew with Equal Rights Arguments

The *Akaka Bill* is born out of the conviction that Native Hawaiians should no longer hold onto a passive role as "wards of the nation [...] dependent on the United States." But every effort to gain the rights to a share in decisions on Hawaiian affairs runs into the opposition of a vocal group of Americans who define such efforts as preferential racial treatment and a threat to their equal rights.

For a diverse coalition of Libertarians, Republicans, and right-wing groups, collective rights are alien to the strict adherence to individual rights in the US Constitution and Bill of Rights. In this view, the *Akaka Bill* results in "Aloha Segregation" and the Office of Hawaiian Affairs, an organization of the Hawaiian state government, symbolizes the preferential treatment of Native Hawaiians.[40] The simmering opposition of this group was brought to the forefront in the nineties when Harold Rice, a self-identified white, sued Governor Cayetano after he was denied the right to vote in the OHA trustee elections in which the right to vote is reserved to native Hawaiians (more than 50% blood quantum) and Hawaiians (less but with clear Hawaiian ancestry). Reversing the judgment of the Federal District Court the US Supreme Court ruled in February 2000 that the voting law for OHA violates the Fifteenth Amendment. The majority of the Court did not deny the unique position of OHA as a trust for the ceded land Congress transmitted to the Hawaiian state government. The majority of the Supreme Court insists that OHA is a state institution – an opinion Native Hawaiian critics of OHA share. Upholding the voting scheme of OHA, Justice Kennedy concludes for the majority, "would be to permit a State, by racial classification, to fence out whole classes of its citizens from decision-making in critical state affairs. The Fifteenth Amendment forbids this result."[41]

What is astonishing about the Supreme Court decision is less that the majority declared the OHA trustee elections unconstitutional. It is the fact that the legal argumentation relies on a dubious mixture of race related arguments, something the judges could have easily avoided. Instead they declare at great length that "ancestry can be a proxy for race. It is that proxy here."[42] Moreover, they interpret the Hawaiian quest for self-determination through the "specialized lens" of the Fifteenth Amendment case law. The lens, Judge Stevens reminded the majority, is "honed in specific detail to reveal the realities of time, place, and history behind the voting restrictions being tested." With their ahistorical equation, Stevens concluded, the majority deliberately ignored "the overwhelming differences [...] between an age of abject discrimination against an insular minority in the old South and the unique history of the State of Hawaii."[43]

The Rice v. Cayetano decision set the tone for further debate. For those opponents of the *Akaka Bill* who perceive collective rights for Native Hawaiians in any form as reverse racial discrimination the Bill became the "Hawaiian race case."[44] OHA is attacked as a "racialist commission" and the demands of Native Hawaiians for self-determination are depicted as a threat to the social fabric of the United States and its Constitution. Three years after the decision, Anne Keala Kelly wrote a column in the *Honolulu Star-Bulletin* condemning the racism in the ruling. "Race is America's blood sport, and its courts will adjudicate with their blood rules, rules constructed as a way to dispossess Hawaiians [...] of their land, resources and if need be, their sanity."[45] For the writer there is no way out of the racial and colonial entanglement as long as Native Hawaiians try to address their demands on the level of the Federal Government. Its dependence on Congressional approval is what makes Kelly an outspoken opponent of the *Akaka Bill*.[46]

Whether the *Akaka Bill* manages to overcome the racial pitfalls which mark American history of the past three hundred years and get a process of reconciliation off the ground remains to be seen. Even if the Bill passes both Houses, its future is not at all secured. In the last round of revisions in December 2009, the Department of Justice already anticipated the scrutiny the Bill will get in the Supreme Court. In addition to the already mentioned criteria a Hawaiian has to fulfill in order to qualify as a Native Hawaiian constituent, the Bill now piles up a whole set of new ones that try to counter the argument that ancestry is a proxy for race.

In order to qualify as a constituent on the membership roll a person now must not only show proof of her Hawaiian descent – as already required in the first version of the Bill in 2000 – and indicate that she "wish[es] to participate in the reorganization of the Native Hawaiian governing entity." She has also to show that she "maintains a significant cultural, social, or civic connection to the Native Hawaiian community."[47] The requirement calls for an active choice to be Hawaiian, and it aims in particular at the large Native Hawaiian population living on the mainland and elsewhere. In other words, an individual has to demonstrate a personal identification as Native Hawaiian, something that is hard to standardize in legal norms. The recent version of the Bill attempts to do just that – to set up objective and unambiguous criteria for identification. The 2009 version lists ten auxiliary criteria, of which two or more can be used as evidence of personal identification as Hawaiian. These include, for instance, place of residency, membership in Hawaiian organizations, and property interest in "*kuleana* land."[48]

Whether this effort to define distinct boundaries of the Native Hawaiian community will be enough to convince the majority of the Supreme Court to grant the Native Hawaiians rights comparable to those the American Indians have is hard to predict. What will not abate in the near future is the 'racialization' of the debate about indigenous rights in the US.

VI. Native Hawaiians and *Akaka*: A New Start or an Extension of the Past?

Victor offered Auntie Eleanor a way of circumventing *Akaka* and its interpretations of sovereignty, identity, and indigeneity. The appeal to a kingdom banished the US and a long history of colonialism from the equation. While Eleanor shared Victor's respect for the Hawaiian kingdom, she regarded it more as a metaphor for 'ancient ways' than as a viable political entity. Victor's references to the throne evoked the glue of past social relations and the values manifested in reciprocity, mutual responsibility, and generosity – or *aloha*. For Eleanor, the kingdom Victor advocated represented the persistence of Hawaiian culture despite colonial intervention, but it was irrelevant to a 'reorganization' of the relation between Hawai`i and the United States.

Eleanor's responses to Victor offer another interpretation of sovereignty. The conversation that afternoon, around the table, prompts a reconsideration of the meanings of identity and indigeneity that attach to sovereignty in public debate and in the *Akaka Bill*. Eleanor disconnected sovereignty from any of the existing proposals for a new governing entity and she deemed the bureaucratic wrangling over criteria for belonging, or membership, irrelevant to the lives of 'ordinary' Hawaiians.

Her interpretation testifies to the persistence of colonial strategies in contemporary discussions of self-determination, identity, and indigeneity. From her point of view, the imposition of administrative criteria – requiring tedious, documented signs of proof – suppresses negotiations of identity that have been part of the experience of Hawaiians ever since Cook introduced the archipelago to strangers, *malihini*, who came and never left. A categorical division, based on inherent traits, ignores the fluidity with which individuals claim affiliation, so that belonging is a matter of choice and circumstance. Their ancestors, Auntie Eleanor explained to her granddaughters, included Portuguese, *haole*, and Chinese. "Not Chinese," one granddaughter laughingly exclaimed, banishing it (temporarily, perhaps) from her own self-identification.

Eleanor also recognized that debate over a governing entity deflects from the real problems facing *kanaka maoli* in the most expensive state of the union. Poverty, lack of education, discrimination in the marketplace, high rates of imprisonment – these are not touched by *Akaka* or by his opponents. The Bill does not propose any concrete response to the fact that numbers of Native Hawaiians are homeless, that Hawaiian youth compose the largest population in the prison system, and that schools in Homestead areas are miserably underserved. Once gambling was thrown out of *Akaka*, forbidden to the proposed entity, nothing was said about the material foundation and modes of distributing resources in the new 'Hawaiian community.'

Opponents of *Akaka*, who claim Hawaiian sovereignty and argue for a governing entity autonomously constituted by the indigenous Hawaiian people and free of Congressional control, equally push aside pragmatic solutions in favor of abstract theories of nationhood.

The *Akaka Bill*, with its bid for reorganization, becomes untenable in the light of historical relations between the United States and Hawai`i. Eleanor was a politically active, resourceful Native Hawaiian person, skilled in dealing with state bureaucracies. But she still shared distrust of the US with the majority of Native Hawaiians, stemming from a long history of deception and legal ploys that resulted in the loss of thousands of acres of land and continue to do so in the twenty-first century. The Bill remains silent about a just settlement over the mishandling of the *Hawaiian Trust* that the US government and the state of Hawai`i administer. The Bill offers nothing more than a process for negotiating with the state and the federal government – and, as Eleanor noted, Native Hawaiians have been tricked by the promise of such *processes* for over two centuries.

John shared a good deal of his sister's interpretation of the sovereignty movement. While Akaka introduced his Bill four years after John's death, the main principles in the proposal had been discussed in the state for decades and John's view of Hawaiian-US relations anticipated subsequent debates.

Like Eleanor, he applied the "conditions" of everyday life as a litmus test for various proposals offered by political activists in the 1990s. All fail, he said in his letters and in our conversations, because none confront the situation of Hawaiians in an American state.[49] Although he did not mention colonialism, his description of the situation detailed the many ways in which an imperial nation deprived Hawaiians of the sources of cultural autonomy. Land, language, and custom fell under the cudgel of "greedy" and "selfish" politicians.

"We are not ready," he told me, criticizing leaders who pushed too fast for sovereignty, whatever its precise form. John regarded the American Indians as a worst-case scenario, but with a sympathy that accentuated his denunciation of administratively designated nationhood as the appropriate response to years of oppression, decimation, and discrimination. Granted the status of nations by Congress, American Indian tribes had lost their independence. John continued: without the means of self-sufficiency, Indians had become wards of the US government, a people dependent on welfare and suffering the loss of culture and language. This was the last thing he wanted for Native Hawaiians, and he saw only potential disaster in an analogous mechanism for acknowledging the "autonomy" of another "indigenous, native people."

In the context of two centuries of colonialism, Clinton's 1993 *Apology* appears empty and the statements in the *Akaka Bill* futile. No more than an *Apology* does the Senator's proposal provide the foundation for restoring autonomy to Native Hawaiians. Rather the Bill specifies terms for identifying as Hawaiian as the prerequisite for constituting a governing entity. Like earlier Congressional decisions, *Akaka* concentrates on categorical descriptions that limit a population in order to justify a revision in US policies regarding Hawai`i. Unlike earlier decisions, the Bill inserts choice, honors self-identification, and avoids ascriptive traits that are redolent of race. The Bill's criteria leave a wide scope for defining identity, while citing the rules of exclusion without which 'community' becomes meaningless.

Yet many Hawaiians object to *Akaka*. Perhaps Auntie Eleanor would have seen in the 2009 version little change from previous incarnations.[50] She might well have read, in the list of criteria, an echo of the convoluted rules established by DHHL regarding claims to Homestead plots. As land commissioner on Hawaii, she had protested publicly against the tangle of regulations in the agency's instructions, a tangle she said discouraged Hawaiians from making any claims at all in regard to land. From her perspective, the bureaucratic regulations imposed by DHHL disconnect Hawaiian 'identity' from the benefits that are due Hawaiian persons.

Regardless of how open *Akaka's* criteria for being Hawaiian are, like DHHL rules they can be interpreted as a limitation on self-identification as Hawaiian. And, as Eleanor claimed about Homestead rules, the criteria create a top-down restriction on who can participate in/enjoy the "newly reorganized governing entity." Faced with quick suspicion of race-based policies in the US, Akaka intended his Bill to forestall any accusation of racism in the designation of a Native Hawaiian community. But bowing to the political context means the Bill is as caught in racial dialogue as were the debates of the late nineteenth and early twentieth centuries. In its efforts to claim collective rights, the Bill inevitably brings race to the forefront, despite the Senator's exclusion of the term and its cognates ('blood' is gone or only embedded in reference to the HHCA criterion). Every claim to collective rights in the contemporary American milieu is deemed preferential racial treatment, therefore unconstitutional. Race still enters all decisions affecting America's relation to the 'native indigenous people' of Hawai`i.

Eleanor criticized DHHL for limiting the petitioners for land through a network of rules. She objected to the 50% blood quantum because it was the most restrictive rule and because the trait was ascriptive rather than acquired. A blood quantum designation denied the flexible and incorporative premises of Hawaiian identity. Race only became an issue when the debate over DHHL rules and OHA regulations was Americanized – engaging in the "blood sport," Kelly described. The *Akaka Bill*, avoiding race, equally constrains identification, denying the "play" across identities John practiced. A "membership roll" and a "Hawaiian community" contradict the "beach crossing" John taught me and the "chop suey" ancestry Auntie Eleanor delineated for her grandchildren.[51] Neither John nor Eleanor denied the significance of Hawaiian "custom" – John composed a *Life Story* to transmit customs to his *`ohana* – but both regarded accommodating to the past as a process of negotiating between Hawaiian-ness and American citizenship. This process has adjusted the relative power of two nations for over three centuries, not a political reorganization but a cultural adjustment.

Talk-stories around the kitchen table suggest that efforts to establish a new governing entity overlook the issues of primary concern to (designated) members. While opponents of *Akaka* on the public stage debate the meanings of nation and the criteria for membership, conversations at home, in malls, and on the beaches concern the benefits owed to a people who still endure the injustices of colonialism – including a designation of who they are.

Akaka demonstrates the difficulties of reconciling the incorporation of Hawai`i into the American legal and political system with a quest for collective rights (and self-determination) for "indigenous, native peoples of the United States." On a broader scale, disputes over the Bill expose the difficulties of asserting sovereignty against a history of colonialism without becoming entangled in the rhetoric and practices of a colonial regime. Victor and other monarchists withdraw from two centuries of intersection between colonizers and colonized, and theirs remains a fringe movement, dramatized in sit-ins at the palace but missing from efforts to reorganize the relations between Hawai`i and the US. Instead reorganization takes place in Washington, DC, where the repeated introduction of a Bill in Congress privileges one interpretation of colonialism and the steps beyond colonialism over others. The *Akaka Bill* responds to a history of colonialism with a plan for reorganization within the purview of the colonizing nation. In the United States, as evident in judiciary revisions of the Bill, an attachment to Congressional power and Federal policies keeps race in the forefront of the outcome. The race-making project of American imperialism continues, limiting the route that can carry Hawai`i beyond colonialism.

Acknowledgements:
First of all, I thank John and Eleanor for the time they took to teach a *malihini* important aspects of Hawaiian culture and history. I thank the other individuals in Hawai`i who talked with me and taught me as well. Thanks to Albrecht Funk, and to the two editors of this volume for reading, revising, and commenting on drafts. All errors are my own.

Notes:

---

[1] I use "American" without North not only because Victor did, but also because it is a conventional reference to the United States.
[2] Jocelyn Linnekin and Lin Poyer, eds., Cultural Identity and Ethnicity in the Pacific (Honolulu: University of Hawai`i Press, 1990); Lilikala Kame`eleihiwa, Native Lands, Foreign Desires (Honolulu: Bishop Museum Press, 1992); Ty P. Kawiki Tengan, Native Men Remade (Chapel Hill: University of North Carolina Press, 2008).
[3] *Haole* refers primarily to whites and sometimes to all outsiders.
[4] Victor did not refer to the overthrow of Queen Lili`uokalani in 1893 as the end of the kingdom, since in his view the kingdom never vanished.
[5] Victor knew my own "genealogy," and I had told him that my father had been the head of the UN legal department.
[6] The official name of the island is Hawaii, but it is usually referred to as the Big Island to distinguish it from the state.
[7] "Beach crossing" is Greg Dening's phrase for the process of moving between cultures and negotiating between one source of identity and another. Greg Dening, Beach Crossings. Voyaging Across Times, Cultures, and Self (Philadelphia: University of Pennsylvania Press, 2004).
[8] I do not claim that John and Eleanor are representative or that, as *kupuna*, they voice the opinions of others. I claim that, as my friends, they offered a distinct perspective on Hawaiian sovereignty and identity, not captured by scholarship that focuses on leaders, public figures, and written documents.
[9] Daniel Akaka is part-Hawaiian and a long-time supporter of Native Hawaiian rights. While the House has been receptive to his arguments, Akaka has repeatedly failed to persuade his fellow senators to pass the Bill.
[10] Senator Akaka, Native Hawaiian Government Reorganization Act approved by Senate Committee, press release, 17 Dec. 2009. In April 2011, the US House of Representatives again passed the Bill; as of this writing, it has not yet gone before the Senate.
[11] See for the debates Eric T. L. Love, Race over Empire. Racism and U.S. Imperialism, 1865-1900 (Chapel Hill: University of North Carolina Press, 2004), Chapters 3 and 4, 73-158.
[12] For an account of American expansionism, see Bruce Cumings, Dominion from Sea to Sea. Pacific Ascendancy and American Power (New Haven: Yale University Press, 2009).
[13] In a hearing in the House of Representatives, Royal Mead for the *Hawaiian Sugar Planters' Association* bluntly stated in 1920: "I do not think there is any contest as to who shall dominate; the white race, the white people, the Americans in Hawaii are going to dominate and will continue to dominate, there is no question about it." Cited from Lawrence H. Fuchs, Hawaii Pono "Hawaii the Excellent." An Ethnic and Political History (Honolulu: Bess Press, 1961), 153.

[14] James G. Blaine to James Comly, the US Minister to Hawaii, Dec. 1881, cited in Love, Race over Empire, 92.
[15] If "the present state of things is allowed to go on," John L. Stevens, the US Minister to Hawai`i wrote back to Washington in 1892, "the Asians will soon be largely preponderate." Ibid., 96.
[16] See Ronald Takaki, Pau Hana. Plantation Life and Labor in Hawaii (Honolulu: University of Hawai`i Press, 1983) and for the perspective of Hawaiian nationalists on the Asian migration to Hawai`i, C. Fujikane and Jonathan Y. Okamura, eds., Asian Settler Colonialism. From Local Governance to the Habits of Everyday Life in Hawai`i (Honolulu: University of Hawai`i Press, 2008).
[17] *Kama`āina*, child of the land, includes *haole* who have been resident for several generations.
[18] The HHCA of 1920 (signed on 9 July 1921) is now part of the Hawai`i State Constitution and still constitutes the basis for the allotment of Homesteads to Native Hawaiians. The epithet of "Native Hawaiians as a dying race" was used as matter of fact statement throughout the late nineteenth and early twentieth centuries. In the discussion of the *Organic Act*, the representative William S. Knox stated: "The Hawaiians are a slowly dying race, fading out, soon to be wiped out from among the peoples of the earth" (Congressional Record, 2 Apr. 1900, 1016). The HHCA was presented as a breath of life for the dying Hawaiian race, see J. Kehaulani Kauanui, Hawaiian Blood. Colonialism and the Politics of Sovereignty and Indigeneity (Durham: Duke University Press, 2008) for the debate on the HHCA.
[19] See Kauanui, Hawaiian Blood, 147-50.
[20] Ibid., 8.
[21] This occurs mainly through programs and funding of community organizations.
[22] Hawaii Revised Statutes S10-2: Office of Hawaiian Affairs. The Office of Hawaiian Affairs list demonstrates how malleable the category of race is; the list contains 17 different definitions of race, varying with the administrative purposes. See Office of Hawaiian Affairs 1996: Appendix: Definitions of Race.
[23] Fuchs, Hawaii Pono, 443.
[24] Ibid.
[25] John Dominis Holt, On Being Hawaiian (Honolulu: Topgallant Press, 1964); William Davenport, "The 'Hawaiian Cultural Revolution'. Some Political and Economic Considerations," American Anthropologist 79 (1969): 1-20; George Kanahele, Ku Kanaka: Stand Tall. A Search for Hawaiian Values (Honolulu: University of Hawai`i Press, 1986); G. Terry Kanalu Young, Rethinking the Native Hawaiian Past (New York: Garland Press, 1998).
[26] Kauanui, Hawaiian Blood, Chapter 6, 171-95; Haunani-Kay Trask, "Kūpa`a `Āina. Native Hawaiian Nationalism in Hawai`i," in From a Native Daughter. Colonialism and Sovereignty in Hawai`i (Monroe, ME: Common Courage Press, 1993), 87-110.

[27] In a Congressional Act "Acknowledging the 100th Anniversary of the Overthrow of the Kingdom of Hawai`i in January 1893."
[28] "A Bill to express the policy of the United States regarding the United States' relationship with Native Hawaiians" (Akaka Bill), 106 Congress, 2d. Session S. 2899, 20 July 2000.
[29] In a series of decisions in the late nineteenth century, the Supreme Court granted Congress broad powers to regulate immigration, to define the relations with Indian tribes, and to govern the newly acquired territories. See for a discussion of these plenary powers Alexander Aleinikoff, Semblances of Sovereignty (Cambridge, Mass.: Harvard University Press, 2002), Chapter 2, 11-38.
[30] Rice v. Cayetano, 528 US 495 (2000), Opinion Kennedy, ad 21.
[31] A typical example for this position is Justice Breyer's concurring opinion in Rice v. Cayetano, 528 US 495 (2000), concurrence, Breyer.
[32] Akaka Bill, 106 Congress, S. 2899, 20 July 2000. Sec. 3.1.
[33] Akaka Bill 2000. Section 1.18 A.
[34] Akaka Bill 2001, 107 Congress, S 746, 6 Apr. 2001, Section 2. 6.
[35] Akaka Bill 2009, 109 Congress, Dec. 2009 S. 1011, Sec. 3 .12.
[36] Benedict Anderson, Imagined Communities. Reflections on the Origin and Spread of Nationalism (New York: Verso, 1991).
[37] One of the ironies of this debate was the role of the *Civil Rights Commission* under the George W. Bush government. Upholding the achievements of the civil rights era of the sixties, anti-discrimination becomes the crucial argument with which the Commission fends off demands to compensate for the past injustices done to Native Hawaiians. See United States Commission on Civil Rights 2006 and the response of the Office of Hawaiian Affairs 2007.
[38] See out of many examples: "The Hawaiian Race," National Review Online, 24 Oct. 2007, http://article.nationalreview.com/331612/the-hawaiian-race/editors (accessed 21 Oct. 2012); or go to the website of the Grassroot Institute in Honolulu, http://www.grassrootinstitute.org (accessed 21 Oct. 2012).
[39] Office of Hawaiian Affairs, Native Hawaiian Government Reorganization Act (Akaka Bill) Dec. 2009, Community Panel – Thursday, 7 Jan. 2010, Questions and Answers, 11 at: http://www.oha.org/index.php?option=com_content&task=view&id=1075&Itemid=224 (accessed 21 Oct. 2012).
[40] See for instance "Aloha Segregation. The Akaka Bill Would Create a Race-Based State in Hawaii," Wall Street Journal, 17 Dec. 2009, A 26.
[41] Kennedy, Ante ad 25. The Fifteenth Amendment reads: "The right of citizens of the United States to vote shall not be denied or abridged by the United States or by any State on account of race, color, or previous condition of servitude."
[42] Ibid., Ad 18.
[43] Rice v. Cayetano, 528 US 495 (2000), dissenting Stevens, ad 20.
[44] Ilya Shapiro, "Hawaii's Race Case," Washington Times, 19 Dec. 2008. For a critical discussion of the race argument, see Judith Rohrer, "'Got Race?' The

Production of Haole and the Distortion of Indigeneity in the Rice Decision," The Contemporary Pacific 18,1 (2006): 1-31.

[45] Kelly in the Honolulu Star-Bulletin, 15 Aug. 2005.

[46] "What I think of the Akaka Bill is that it's the United States government – state and federal governments – attempting to further confuse people and lie to people and cover up the fraudulence of the U.S. presence in Hawaii, the fact that it's an illegal occupation," she wrote on 20 February 2010, after the House passed the *Akaka Bill.*

[47] Akaka Bill 2009, 109 Congress, Dec. 2009 S. 1011, Sec. 3 .12 B.

[48] *Kuleana* land refers to the plots granted to Hawaiian petitioners through the HHCA. *Kuleana* translates as "taking responsibility" or caring for.

[49] Judith Schachter, "One Hundred Percent Hawaiian. Life Stories, Politics, and Anthropology," Anthropology and Humanism 35,1 (2010): 81-97.

[50] Eleanor died in December 2008.

[51] "Chop suey" is used widely in Hawai`i to indicate the mixed backgrounds of a majority of residents of the state.

Subject Citizen: The Ambiguity of Citizenship and its Colonial Laboratories

Serhat Karakayali

According to a model of imperial space developed in colonial studies, the activities of colonial powers in the colonial territories are interwoven with societies in their "motherland" in two ways. First, according to the ideology of the "white man's burden," the motherland had to stimulate social, cultural, and political change in the colonial societies, thereby creating a unified image of themselves as "the West" separated from "the rest" by an unbridgeable civilizational gap. Second, colonial space simultaneously functioned as a laboratory or testing ground for modern techniques of social control. The reason behind this was the widespread notion that these spaces represented areas in which less or no legal, social, and political inhibitions existed that hampered scientific progress. In other words, the colonies were regarded as permanent "states of exception."[1] The experiences and technologies developed there then entered a transnational, social and political space, ultimately flowing back to the motherland and influencing the perception and treatment of political and social problems in the metropoles.

In this article, I will argue that the laboratory paradigm must be expanded.[2] It contains two basic assumptions which undermine its usefulness in explaining the interconnection between the development of modern societies in both the metropole and the colonies. First, it relies on a binary structure that underestimates the internal contradictions and differences within the societies of the European colonial powers and within those of the colonized. Second, it does not take into account that the laboratory conditions existed often only in the minds of the colonizers.[3] More significantly, the supposedly passive objects of social and medical experimentation resisted colonizing practices and technologies – a fact which became most obvious with the start of the independence movements. By referring to the example of urban planning debates and practices in Northern Africa during the French colonial period in the twentieth century, I will argue that colonial rule itself can only be understood in a relationalist perspective. Power is a form of structuring agency and is shaped at the same time by the resistance and countervailing power. Trying to escape power reframes power.

In the early 1920s, the first resident-general of Morocco, Hubert Lyautey, contrasted the "unbureaucratic" feasibility of urban construction plans directly with the legal constraints prevailing in France, a country that he considered "lost" to technical and civil progress for this very reason. His attitude reveals a desire for an authoritarian state that Lyautey shared with many members of the French (and European) elite, such as the head of the *Service du Contrôle des Municipalités du Maroc*, Hubert de la Casinière. Both believed that the efficiency of the planning laws in the French North African protectorate was due to the colony's "independence" from the "randomness of democratic elections."[4] The laboratory of the colony had an addressee, namely democracy – in other words, the integration of subaltern groups in the metropole! The laboratory situation based on depriving the colonized of their rights also reflected the tense relationship between democracy, planning, and statehood in Western societies. As Paul Rabinow succinctly noted, "[i]f there was a civilizing mission, its target was the French."[5]

The ambivalence of the process of modernization in general and of the colonial projects in particular becomes apparent when considered in relation to the state. Understanding power from a relationalist perspective means tracing forms of governance, for example the state form, as modes of regulating struggles. Since the end of the nineteenth century, the state was no longer just a liberal night watchman state, but was increasingly regarded as a mediator of social conflicts by implementing insurance technologies, social and urban planning projects.[6] The ambivalent character of state planning as social reform on the one hand and as "managing committee" of the bourgeoisie (as Marx and Engels have called it) on the other can also be found in the colonial context. The settlement projects in Casablanca and other cities oscillated between claiming to be an endeavor of socio-utopian modernization (*Cité Verticale*) and recognizing the "traditional" social structures (*Cité Horizontale*) of those whose social environment had been colonized. The plans of the *Atelier des Batisseurs*, the *ATBAT-Afrique*, differentiated the facades and structures of the *Cité Verticale* in a culturally specific manner and were only realized on a small scale. Meanwhile, the industrially mass-produced grids that served as a horizontal strategy for the mobile labor force in the so-called *bidonvilles* (shantytowns) can be found throughout North Africa and Israel, where they have been employed for building Arab settlements.

In North Africa, the development of new planning procedures was intended to take this ambivalence of the state into consideration. Unlike classical modernism, planners in North Africa based their designs on the living conditions and needs of the people. What was new, and indeed almost revolutionary in the world of architecture, was the careful study of slums in order to discover traces of functioning social structures in the settlements. These would then be integrated into the architects' designs. The social organization of space – meaning its temporary and flexible use, as observed by the *International Congress of Modern Architecture* (CIAM) architects in the *bidonvilles* – was integrated into the planning discourse and the actual realization of the plans for the new settlements' architecture.[7] This example of urban planning demonstrates the double-sided nature of the colonial project, caught in the rift between different characteristics of modern state planning. On the one hand it treated the colonized as a social group that was to be economically modernized, just as Europeans were.[8] On the other hand, the promise of social mobility was broken by racist discrimination, because French colonial law created a fundamental inequality between so called European, Muslim and Jewish people in North Africa.

This ambivalence may be grasped by discussing the concept of "class racism" as proposed by Étienne Balibar. With this term, Balibar describes the intersections and entanglements created by class struggles in capitalist nation-states.[9] A similar argument, but with regard to the social history of Great Britain, is made by Michael Hechter, who speaks of "internal colonialism," describing the development of a new form of ethnicity ("the Celtic") in conjunction with class positioning.[10] Hechter demonstrates that in the nineteenth century, during the development of the industrial proletariat, a new ethnification of socio-economic differences took root. Before the emergence of capitalist industrialization and for a long time afterwards, concepts such as race, class or nationality were not unambiguously distinguished from one another, but instead were applied equally to various social groups. The most significant attribute of these groups was that they were regarded as endogamous population groups. Historically the concept of race was ethnicized only with the emergence of the nation-state, as Balibar argues. Based on these observations race and racism are far from "substituting" class or being "used" as an ideological weapon against representations of society based on class concepts. Rather class and race represent two poles "of a permanent dialectic, which is at the heart of modern representations of history."[11]

These forms of racism were exacerbated by what Michel Foucault has called "biopolitics." Workers were regarded as members of the *classes dangereuses*,[12] who supposedly threatened the very stability of society itself. They were seen as a source of disease and criminality and, most of all, of possible political revolt. In the course of the nineteenth century, however, the mode of class conflict was successfully altered. In contrast to traditional liberalists, social reformists and an increasingly strong labor movement were able to establish the idea, according to François Ewald, that "the social" was a separate entity that could and had to be regulated to the benefit of the whole society.[13] At the individual level, this regulation included improved education and schooling. As such, it served as a kind of transmission belt between the various social divisions of labor and their consequences. Based on the postulate of equality, these technologies of social and individual improvement simultaneously "regulated" the smooth transition between class differences and enabled workers to become socially and politically integrated as citizens over the course of the nineteenth century.

Thus, the naturalization of the working classes as citizens was a question of education, upbringing, and discipline, in short: governing their behavior. The workers were to be formed into worker-citizens through various social techniques such as worker settlements.[14] Workers had to be taught to show up for work on time, to not miss work on Mondays, and to run an "orderly" household. The central aim of disciplining policies was to tie the workers to the workplace right from the beginning of the industrial mode of production.[15]

Here, we find a structural similarity between modern class racism and colonial racism. The technologies and strategies employed in both cases oscillate between fixating groups according to biological characteristics on the one hand, and facilitating social mobility and change by educational programs on the other.

For European workers, the rise of the modern nation-state and the class compromise was a way to join a community of (at least formally) equals. Yet, workers were simultaneously regarded by the hegemonic bourgeoisie as a foreign race. During the course of the nineteenth century and the process of nationalization and colonization, however, the "borders of nationality" shifted: social groups at the legal and political margins of the state were each attributed a different legal status. Members of the so-called under classes could not move as freely within the borders of the German Reich, for example, as members of other groups. Although different measures were taken to facilitate mobility ("Passkarten-Abkommen," or the "Right to Emigrate," granted by the constitutional Assembly of 1848) it was the fact that the German Reich around 1850 still was departmentalized in dozens of legal territories that allowed the authorities to restrict legal mobility for certain groups who were regarded "untrustworthy."[16]

I. The Structural Logic of Violence

In concepts of rationalization based on the ideas of Max Weber, as well as in many state and dominance theories within the tradition of Marx's *Critique of Political Economy*, state violence appears either as an atavist relic or as an exception in crises threatening the system. Coercion is regarded as a subsidiary means of domination. This contrasts with an emphasis on the mute coercion of circumstances and its legal "superstructure," which increasingly represses all non-economic violence in a way that is virtually synonymous with pre-capitalist circumstances. Following Marx, Étienne Balibar considers the "non-coincidence of labour and surplus labour" the criterion for the difference between feudal and capitalist modes of production, which makes the use of "non-economic measures for effectively executing surplus labour necessary."[17] In the feudal mode of production, the absorption of surplus labor consequently assumes the form of domination and slavery. Thus, while the absorption of the surplus product is transformed into an economic process, the coercion of the labor force changes its form rather than vanishes.

Colonialism is probably the best proof that the various forms of slavery and serfdom spread primarily with the development and expansion of capitalism. In the modern age they were the most important institutions of immobilizing the labor force through coercive means. With the rise of the nation-state as a "national social" state, the contradictions in the field of conflict of mobility were partially "resolved" through the incorporation of social rights. Where restrictions in mobility receded, economic rationalities were conversely employed and shifted the moments of coercion to the newly emerging national borders of the state.[18]

In this context, it is important to note that the freedom from conflict claimed as an achievement by liberalism is not the result of the capitalist mode of production, but rather the outcome of the historical battles of the labor movement. Within the Northern hemisphere, social struggles over the course of several centuries have led to the compromises by the democratic and social welfare state that we commonly refer to as civil rights, among which are labor rights. Not only did unions and other labor organizations engage in economic crusades concerning working hours and wages, but they also dealt with questions of individual freedom. In Britain, for instance, the battle over the limitation of freedom of contract was closely connected to the development and crystallization of freedom of person:[19] "Modern free labor in England must be seen as a product of labor's struggle to improve its position in a market society."[20]

This market-oriented view that took the nation-state as the limit of its market resulted in an element of boundary-drawing within the labor movement itself. The central question was: Who belonged to the working class, and who was excluded from it? This question was resolved by including white, male workers into the working masses and excluding "foreign" workers and women. Thus, the violent aspects of labor force policies discussed above also permeated the social struggles and created the minority labor force of the immigrant.[21] As a consequence, the formation of nations brought about a literal identification and symbolic unification of "the people," by which each individual was equipped with identification papers tying him or her to a national space and turning all of them into the nation's population.

II. Colonialism and Anthropology

In the colonial territories, post-war modernity, namely the critical paradigm shift from the "housing machine" to the "habitat," takes place under the conditions of a colonial regime of education and governance, in which the political and economic conditions in the metropole are negotiated at the same time. Of course, this "negotiation" is conducted with the overwhelming non-participation of the colonized subjects. In the numerous references to architecture and housing practices from "the South" developed in the 1960s, the colonized are usually only objects of study rather than subjects of design.[22] Moreover, the idea of "learning from" did not confront the specific constellation of power in which the architectural designs emerged. Instead, "learning" oscillated between a discourse of recognition, which was critical of modernity, and culturalistic patterns of interpretation, which makes it possible to bridge the experiences of colonialism or the "colonial situation" via the indirect route of anthropology.

Modernity is, since its early beginnings, founded on the fundamental distinction between the "modern" and the "traditional." Since Jean Jacques

Rousseau's writings, the concept of "the primitive" has played a central role in modern Western thought. Whereas the figure of the "barbarian" represented the spatially defined Other in ancient Greece, modernity's Other was increasingly defined by a temporal difference.[23] Consequently, the narrative of the "traditional society" represented a founding myth of capitalist modernity and of colonialism alike.[24]

However, several problems were inherent to the process of anthropologization, rendering its outcome uncertain and contingent. First, it permitted social practices that colonialism or Eurocentrism had previously coded as negative to be regarded as valuable in their own right. Characteristics of the colonized were, in what could be framed in Ulrich Beck's terminology as a second modernity within architectural discourse, now described as universally human. The critique of modernity, including the critique of certain effects of functional differentiation or standardization, was opposed to ways of life that seemed to be unaffected of these pathologies. How were these universally human characteristics created?

As indicated by the term itself, this involves a general abstraction from local contexts. Within the context of colonialism and its ideologies of superiority and progress, this abstraction nevertheless simultaneously legitimized colonial domination: local cultures were relics of a pre-modern past that had to be overcome. The less "developed" cultures were, the earlier they were to be located on the time axis. This construction theoretically and sometimes also practically implied that the members of the local cultures placed themselves on the timeline of modernity. Improvement and progress, however, were thought to be possible only under the instruction and guidance of the already modernized Europeans. It should also be noted at this point that not all Europeans automatically met this claim to superiority made by colonial discourse. So-called "poor whites" undermined the image of the master race in many colonies, and were, as historians have shown, partly deported or forced into labor camps, for example in colonial India.[25]

In the French protectorate of Morocco, the resident-general Hubert Lyautey had implemented a policy of cultural separation since the 1920s. According to the French colonial paradigm of saving "local cultures" from contamination and conserving them for the future, for instance, Christians in Morocco were forbidden to enter mosques. Generally, throughout the entire northern African territory under French control, a religiously coded system of apartheid between white French settlers and colonized Africans was installed.

Considering these findings, we have to reevaluate the aforementioned project of a "local" version of modernity, which was especially designed to take existing cultural characteristics into account. As my thoughts on the anthropologization have demonstrated, modernist architectural projects were deeply embedded in colonial discourse and were entangled in a number of contradictions right from its start. To give an example: Georges Candilis, who was involved in constructing "culture-specific housing" in settlement projects in Casablanca during the 1950s, proposed three categories: Muslims, Jews, and "Europeans" (by which the authorities understood white Christian settlers).[26]

Yet, a new discourse developed in Europe and in the West – critical to the paradigms of modernity – and took over the "politics of the time." It gained prominence and inverted existing paradigms. Modernity was now decoded critically and was interpreted as alienation, exploitation or capitalism; it was possible to enhance the status of pre-modern ways of living. To some extent, the architectural debates are only one example of the many discourses crystallizing since the 1960s, in which the people of the Global South became a point of reference. These could be seen as some version of the Deleuzian "devenir minoritaire," the desire to escape majoritarian forms of subjectivation.[27] This new discourse surrounding the critique of modernity was, however, an oppositional, a non-hegemonic one.

The fact that the "other modernism" was based on a relationship of learning from non-European cultures spurred the opponents of this critique of modernity in the discursive war of positions. Just as the critics of the power relationships of modernity referred positively to the primal humanness of the Others, those whom the critique addressed could also refer to the still dominant negative coding. The most prominent example is probably the montage of Bedouins and camels into a photograph of the Weissenhof settlement in Stuttgart, created in 1932 and widely distributed by the Nazis in the 1940s.[28]

As previously mentioned, the "discovery" of the traditional cultural practices of building and the implementation of these practices in the European mode of mass construction were successful because the techniques "discovered" by the architects and planners were embedded in a complex social assemblage. Its success relied on the notion of modernization, shared by proponents of colonialism and activists of the anticolonial movement alike. Both, however, ignored the local contexts of the practices involved. This becomes all the more problematic as this form of modernist thought omits the political dimension of the cultural practices in question. It sidesteps the tactical and strategic function of identity-related narrations, and therefore results in an alternation between essentialism on the one hand and the promise of universalism on the other. To avoid these pitfalls, it is vital to interpret cultural forms as vehicles and sites of social struggles. Cultural practices – even certain modes of living or settling – are permeated by power.

If we apply this perspective to analyze the urban planning projects in colonial North Africa, it becomes apparent that the practice of the *bidonvilles* involves moving in different socio-political spaces, thereby changing the spaces and people involved. It represents a commonplace practical form of engagement with the colonial economy. Yet simultaneously, it also demonstrates the generative force of migration as movement, which had multiple effects: First, it challenges the foundations of governance on a biopolitical level, because it constantly changes the composition of populations. This means that cultural and social practices are also exposed to a constant reconfiguration, which has to be regulated, and to which the colonial and metropolitan governments must react again and again.

Second, migration itself is a form of modernity, as it represents a self-reliant, individual form of political practice, the exodus. Flight or exit has to be seen as a fundamental political strategy within asymmetric relationships of power, in which migrants are always embedded. Originally, the current model of an ordinary, free relationship based on a wage or salary was that of conquest. The former non-free and binding commercial or indenture contract was transformed into a labor contract for an undetermined duration, incorporating the right to escape.[29] Escape and flight can be seen as a form of resistance against these situations of inequality. As a consequence, the search for autonomy and liberty has produced powerful institutional effects.

One might argue that in the eyes of administrations in general migrants represent nothing more than objects of control and that the asymmetric relationship proves the predominance of the rulers. To counter balance this view, it might be useful to take into consideration the perspective of the actor-network theory in which "objects" reclaim their rights as actors. The *bidonvilles* in Casablanca, for instance, were also breeding grounds for anticolonial resistance, in which many of those involved locally inscribed themselves into the European Western discourse of modernity.

The perspective of a political anthropology can also be applied to the act of translation, the learning from the so called primitive, which distills a kind of primal human self-organization from the *bidonvilles* and other forms of settlement. We know from the theory of hegemony that every particular interest requires a generalization to become capable of hegemony. Hegemonic policies, as suggested by Ernesto Laclau, must make use of an empty signifier, which also enables other groups to inscribe themselves into what is newly shared. From this view, whatever is anthropological or inherently human is an abstraction, which should make it possible to merge social practices in order to create a fundamental change by dealing with what non-Europeans and Europeans have in common on neutral ground.[30]

Yet, one objection to this concept stands out: there might be a particularity of the *situation coloniale* that is less imaginary than material and that is held in common. Colonization is a permanent process of the total modernization of society, which is applied to Europeans and non-Europeans in different ways. The fundamental rift of modernity, its unfulfilled promise of total autonomy and equality, manifests itself in the dichotomy of citizen and subject. Whether relying on the purist claim for autonomy or the redesign of the relationship between governance and sovereignty, the antinomy between promise and reality will still persist. Seen in this context, the practice of architects and planners represents the nation-state's perspective on governing the multitudes: directing and redirecting its flows and molding its behaviors.

Accordingly, each urban housing project can be regarded as a technique of biopolitical governance. Yet, each population subjected to one of these projects reacted differently to modes of modernist governance ranging from the appropriation of buildings or structures to open resistance to settlement policies. In his long-term study of the resettlement of the inhabitants of the *bidonville* of Ben M'sick, Abdelmajid Arrif coined the phrase of "dialogue souterrain" to describe its twofold result.[31] Not only did concepts of modernism and urban planning circulate within the transnational space between metropole and colonies, but also ways and means to react to this form of biopolitics. One of the examples Arrif mentions is the case of "Ben M'sick/Hay MoulayRachid, Bethnal Green/Greenleigh et le 13ème arrondissement de Paris:" Peter and Alison Smithson, members of the Team X which built the Robin Hood Gardens housing estate in the London district of Bethnal Green, were also involved in the *bidonville* Ben M'Sick. Hence, apart from the historical and conceptual connection between metropolitan and colonial urban planning projects, there is another level on which it makes sense to think of a dialogue between these places.

Today, however, this dialogue is no longer underground. The struggles around migration in France and elsewhere in Europe clearly show that the colonial relationship is far from being a historical relic. The organization *Indigènes de la République*, founded after the riots of 2005, spells out the intrinsic relation between the modern institution of the republic and colonial domination. It is possible that this leads on to envisioning the technologies of power which result in the production of this difference. Instead of reifying the identitarian categories that result from these procedures, focusing on the power technologies might serve as a better foundation for a critique of modernity.

III. Conclusion

Colonial modernity was considered to be a testing ground for new discourses of modernization and for the large housing programs that were installed throughout Europe and the colonies after the war, to reinforce the creation of a global Fordism. As Marion von Osten has emphasized, it is no coincidence that these processes and global decolonization were taking place simultaneously. The ability to plan was questioned by a generation of architects in the West, who were interested in the everyday, the popular. By discovering the so called ordinary aesthetics, they encouraged a new relationship to the constructed environment.[32] In her critique of the "learning from" approach, von Osten claims that in fact the architects "learned" little from the everyday practices of the inhabitants, but rather adopted the concept of the typical European nuclear family. This resulted in a hybrid (or a compromise, in terms of political theory) between colonial modernity and culturally specific conceptions. What was obviously not conceivable for Western planners was the specifically urban, that is *modern* character of the self-built environment, which was already a means of coping with both modern city life and colonial subordination. Ultimately, "learning from" the dwellers was merely a matter of adjusting their planning according to ethnological findings. In fact, anticolonial movements and the everyday life of the colonized operated as "irritations,"[33] to use Niklas Luhmann's words, acting as an external stimulus to self-referentially closed systems within societies. Planning absorbed the stimulants of anticolonialism and the lives of the colonized as a form of information, which in turn was translated into planning's own rationality.

In a critical theory of social relations, this process would be designated "absorption," for example in Herbert Marcuse's critique of late capitalist culture. Luc Boltanski and Eve Chiapello have recently put this Marxist perspective back on the theoretical agenda.[34] Marx established the theory that capitalism needs, in order to reproduce its cycles of production and consumption, an obscure and rather ghostly substance (living labor). Today, it seems, this process has reached a new stage in which not only the everyday life of people has become part of those cycles through mass consumption, but also other spheres such as thoughts, behaviors, social interactions, networks, etc. New concepts such as "immaterial labor"[35] and "cognitive capitalism"[36] try to grasp these new developments. However, Boutang, Hardt, and Negri would disagree with Marcuse and maybe also with Marx in one point: absorption does not equal "destruction" or negation, to use the Hegelian terminology. Appropriating elements of the social is a process of dismembering it, and in a sense, dismembering is destruction. Here it is useful to remember the "antihumanist" line of reasoning spanning from Marx to Nietzsche, to Althusser and to Foucault, in which emancipation can be understood as the rejection and destruction of the human and its subjectivity. Thinking of "people" rather than of assemblages (as Deleuze and others extensively did) leads to a different assessment regarding what we have called "learning from" the poor, the colonized, or the vernacular. It is true that urban planners have dismembered the social in order to "digest" what could be integrated into their planning strategies. But if we think of the social as a realm composed of different and manifold entities (bodies, language, ideas, buildings, etc.), we see that social struggles such as anticolonialism still persist. They have radically changed their appearance and they have been inscribed onto a new plane, but the theoretical task of today is not to mourn a historical loss, but to engage in mapping those new planes of cognitive and biopolitical capitalism, and to identify the current arenas of battle.

Notes:

---

1 Giorgio Agamben, Ausnahmezustand, trans. Ulrich Müller-Schöll (Frankfurt am Main: Suhrkamp, 2004). On a conceptual level recently argued also against by Arjun Chowdhury, "The Colony as Exception (Or, Why Do I Have to Kill You More than Once?)," borderlands ejournal 6,3 (2007): 35, http://www.borderlands.net.au/vol6no3_2007/chowdhury_once.htm (accessed 21 Oct. 2012).

---

[2] I argue here in conjunction with a number of other scholars such as Frederick Cooper und Ann Laura Stoler, "Between Metropole and Colony. Rethinking a Research Agenda," in Tensions of Empire. Colonial Cultures in a Bourgeois World, eds. eid. (Berkeley: University of California Press, 1997), 1-56; Dirk van Laak, "Kolonien als 'Laboratorien der Moderne'?" in Das Kaiserreich transnational. Deutschland in der Welt 1871-1914, eds. Jürgen Osterhammel and Sebastian Conrad (Göttingen: Vandenhoeck & Ruprecht, 2004), 257-79, 258.

[3] As van Laak also points out in "Kolonien als 'Laboratorien der Moderne'," 259.

[4] Paul Rabinow, French Modern. Norms and Forms of the Social Environment (Cambridge, Mass.: MIT Press, 1989), 291.

[5] Rabinow, French Modern, 291.

[6] Jacques Donzelot, "L'invention du social," Vingtième siècle. Revue d'histoire 5 (1985): 198-9; François Ewald, "Die Versicherungs-Gesellschaft," Kritische Justiz 4 (1989): 385-93. See also James C. Scott, Seeing Like a State. How Certain Schemes to Improve the Human Condition Have Failed (New Haven: Yale University Press, 1998), 103-46.

[7] See Alison Smithson, Team 10 Primer (Cambridge, Mass.: MIT Press, 1968).

[8] In fact, both colonialism and modernization aimed at inducing an overall social process that, at least theoretically, was directed at Europeans and non-Europeans alike.

[9] Étienne Balibar and Immanuel Wallerstein, Race, Class, Nation. Ambiguous Identities (London: Verso, 1991).

[10] Michael Hechter, Internal Colonialism. The Celtic Fringe in British National Development, 1536-1966 (Berkeley: University of California Press, 1975).

[11] Balibar and Wallerstein, Race, Class, Nation, 207.

[12] Piers Beirne, Inventing Criminology. Essays on the Rise of Homo Criminalis (Albany: State University of New York Press, 1993), 69.

[13] François Ewald, L'état providence (Paris: B. Grasset, 1986).

[14] Hubert Treiber and Heinz Steinert, Die Fabrikation des zuverlässigen Menschen. Über die Wahlverwandtschaft von Kloster- und Fabrikdisziplin (München: Moss, 1980).

[15] Robert Castel, Les métamorphoses de la question sociale. Une chronique du salariat (Paris: Fayard, 1995).

[16] Alf Lüdtke, "Gemeinwohl", Polizei und "Festungspraxis." Staatliche Gewaltsamkeit und innere Verwaltung in Preussen, 1815-1850 (Göttingen: Vandenhoeck & Ruprecht, 1982).

[17] Étienne Balibar, Das Kapital lesen, mit Louis Althusser (Reinbek bei Hamburg: Rowohlt, 1972), 296.

[18] Serhat Karakayali, Gespenster der Migration (Bielefeld: transcript, 2008), Chapter 2.

[19] The workers were fighting for limitations to contracts because cases of breach of contract between employers and workers frequently led to criminal proceedings in the nineteenth century. See Robert J. Steinfeld, Coercion, Contract, and Free Labor in the Nineteenth Century (Cambridge: Cambridge University Press, 2001).
[20] Steinfeld, Coercion, Contract, and Free Labor, 234.
[21] Karakayali, Gespenster der Migration.
[22] See Marion von Osten, "Architecture without Architects – Another Anarchist Approach," e-flux Journal 6, 05/2009, http://www.e-flux.com/ journal/view/59 (accessed 21 Oct. 2012).
[23] Hayden White, Tropics of Discourse. Essays in Cultural Criticism (Baltimore: Johns Hopkins University Press, 1978); Reinhart Koselleck, Vergangene Zukunft. Zur Semantik geschichtlicher Zeiten (Frankfurt am Main: Suhrkamp, 1979); Johannes Fabian, Time and the Other. How Anthropology Makes Its Object (New York: Columbia University Press, 2002).
[24] Peter Wehling, Die Moderne als Sozialmythos (Frankfurt am Main: Campus, 1992).
[25] Minu Haschemi Yekani, "Fragmenting the Colonial Order. (Un)Wanted Migration in German East Africa." Paper presented at "Germany and the World in the Age of Globalization. Migration, Mobility and Movement in Modern German History," Cambridge, 29-31 March 2011; Harald Fischer-Tiné, "Englands interne Zivilisierungsmission. Arbeitshäuser für Europäer im kolonialen Indien (ca. 1860-1914)," in Zivilisierungsmissionen. Imperiale Weltverbesserung seit dem 18. Jahrhundert, eds. Boris Barth and Jürgen Osterhammel (Konstanz: UVK Verlagsgesellschaft, 2005), 169-200, 172.
[26] Jean-Louis Cohen and Monique Eleb, Casablanca. Colonial Myth and Architectural Ventures (New York: Monacelli Press, 2002).
[27] Gilles Deleuze and Félix Guattari, Capitalisme et schizophénie. Mille plateaux (Paris: Éditions de Minuit, 1980).
[28] The photomontage was created as early as 1932 and became well known due to its distribution by the Nazis in the 1940s.
[29] Yann Moulier Boutang, De L'esclavage au salaria. Economie historique du salariat bridé (Paris: Presse Universitaire de France, 1998); Paolo Virno, "About Exodus," Grey Room 21 (2005): 17-20.
[30] Ernesto Laclau, "Why Constructing a People Is the Main Task of Radical Politics," Critical Inquiry 32,4 (2006): 646-80.
[31] Abdelmajid Arrif, "Fragments d'une enquête dans un bidonville de Casablanca," Ethnologie française 31,1 (2001): 29-39.
[32] von Osten, "Architecture without Architects."
[33] Niklas Luhmann, "Die Behandlung von Irritationen. Abweichung oder Neuheit?" in Gesellschaftsstruktur und Semantik. Studien zur Wissenssoziologie der modernen Gesellschaft. Band 4, id. (Frankfurt am Main: Suhrkamp, 1995), 55-100.

[34] Herbert Marcuse, One-Dimensional Man. Studies in the Ideology of Advanced Industrial Society (Boston: Beacon Press, 1963); Luc Boltanski and Eve Chiapello, The New Spirit of Capitalism (London: Verso, 2005).
[35] Michael Hardt and Toni Negri, Empire (Cambridge, Mass.: Harvard University Press, 2000); Maurizio Lazzarato, Immaterial Labour, http://www.generation-online.org/c/fcimmateriallabour3.htm (accessed 21 Oct. 2012); Christian Marazzi, "Rules for the Incommensurable," SubStance 112, 36,1 (2007): 11-36.
[36] Yann Moulier Boutang, Le capitalisme cognitive. La nouvelle grande transformation (Paris: Edition Amsterdam, 2008).

Connecting some Dots: Migration, Colonialism, and Questions of Citizenship in Postcolonial Europe

Manuela Bojadžijev

I would like to begin my paper by referring to an apodictic and foresighted comment made by the German Federation of Trade Unions (*Deutscher Gewerkschaftsbund*) at an event in Nuremberg in 1974. Referring to migrant movements in European countries since the 1950s, the Union formulated: "the foreign worker is the European citizen of tomorrow. The European worker precedes the European citizen."[1] This vision implied an anticipation that would soon prove to be a very astute observation: migration would not only contribute to the making of Europe but would do so in an ambiguous manner. Generally speaking, migration movements to Europe from both the European peripheries as well as from former or (at this time) still existent colonies challenged the social and political make-up of countries of immigration in a twofold way. On the one hand, inhabitants of colonial territories were struggling for national independence via anti-colonial movements, which resulted in a limitation of Europe's colonial power and a necessity to re-invent herself constitutionally and politically. On the other hand, migrants from both former colonies and the peripheries of Europe alike formed political organizations in order to improve their living and working conditions and to support anti-colonial liberation movements in their home countries, often by ways of exile politics.

Whether such migrant aspirations eventually created "European citizens" has remained disputed until today. In light of the current and persistent European crisis, the existence of such a "citizenship in Europe," as recently suggested by Étienne Balibar,[2] seems even more unlikely than ever before. Moreover, the utopian idea that migration eventually created "European citizens" has already receded into the background by 1974, the year of the Union's rendition. But this vision, that migration would produce "European citizens," already began to fade in 1974, the year of its promulgation. Certainly, this was the case more than the new composition of the population of Europe might have suggested, given how this was affected by the movements of migration. 1974, the year of the Trade Union's utopian proclamation, was also the year when most European immigration countries set the course for new immigration policy. Such countries include the Federal Republic of Germany, France, Belgium, the Netherlands (all members of the *European Economic Community*), as well as Great Britain and Austria. Although proceeding in an uncoordinated fashion, they all discontinued the former practice of organized, contract-based recruitment of migrants, thereby heralding the end of a period, which in Germany until today is known as the era of the "Gastarbeiter" (guest worker).[3] It is, however, important to keep in mind that these decisions were embedded in specific historical and political contexts and are characterized by significant differences. In Britain, for instance, citizenship rights throughout the Commonwealth guaranteed migrants access to the same political rights in the UK. Migration to Germany, on the contrary, always implied crossing a national border without such a shared legal framework and notions of a transnational community therefore always resulted in the disenfranchisement of the migrant.

It is the aim of this paper to integrate the history of colonialism and migration into the history of the constitution of Europe and European civil rights. I will argue that transnational migration is a vital and characteristic element of the history of what we consider to be understood as a European identity. It determines its potential as well as its limitations. Central to the emergence of this identity are mechanisms of inclusion and exclusion. Often, the inclusive concept of civil rights translated into an inclusive exclusion, namely the inclusion into the national fold as second class citizens. Balibar drastically calls this practice the "recolonialization of migration."[4] On the following pages, I will investigate to what extent contemporary Europe can be regarded as a postcolonial formation starting from the observation of the persistent influence of an ever shifting and permanently renewed migratory movement.[5] It is this migratory movement that can be considered the material basis for an entangled history that resonates precisely in the term post-colonial. To elaborate on my theoretical considerations, which are inspired by British academic debates on migration, I focus on the case of Germany, which is a neglected aspect in the research and scholarship on migration and postcolonialism.

I. Entanglement and Struggles: A Double Perspective European History

Shalini Randeria and Sebastian Conrad developed one way to approach this gap in the scholarship, which is to analyze local histories and its global interconnectedness. These scholars describe European history as an "entangled history" and discuss several characteristics of this entanglement.[6] The first and foremost among them is the fact that Europe is the product of a shared and divided history. Shared in terms of a common history and divided in a topographical, metaphorical sense – two separated histories of the North and the South. According to Randeria and Conrad, the challenge of an entangled history is narrating these two shared/divided histories simultaneously. Despite this challenge, this approach acknowledges the legacy of European colonialism, including all repercussions of colonialism inscribed into the societies of up until the present. Moreover, it avoids the methodological nationalism that in the past has often narrowed our analyses.

Investigating the history of entanglement means to conduct problem-oriented research instead of choosing a fixed analytical starting point. Problem-oriented research allows us to focus on entanglements in time and space, instead of privileging national space, territoriality, civilizations or cultures. This research conceptualizes national or cultural spaces as the products of historical entanglements. Following Randeria's and Conrad's suggestions, we would head for a relational perspective that offers an analytical framework to understand the entanglements and interactions through which Europe as an entity emerged. Simultaneously, this approach enables us to analyze not only the formation of a European identity but also the formation of identity for its constitutive 'Others.'

I would like to complement Randeria's and Conrad's approach with a special emphasis on the analysis of both the anti-colonial struggles outside of Europe as well as the struggles of migrants within Europe itself. The resulting double perspective allows us to reconstruct the shared/divided Europe while simultaneously considering the production of Europe and its 'Others' as political entities. As such, Europe's entangled history is no longer simply a relational one but a narrative of interconnected, shared, and (in some cases) dividing political struggles – struggles of anti-colonial movements and of migrants alike. To determine the relationships between these two movements, both contested and structured by power, is a central task of such a twofold approach. After all, it were these struggles and movements that contributed to the discontinuity of colonialism and racism. Based on these considerations, I would like to introduce the concept of postcolonialism into critical migration research.

II. Common Denial: Public Perception of the History of Colonialism and Migration

Postcolonialism, although well established in the Anglophone academic world, is generally received with great reluctance in Germany, with a few exceptions. This corresponds to the even slower start of a historical migration research that focuses on Germany as an immigration country. Additionally, both fields of research still have to define their mutual relationship. This neglect is even more tangible in non-scholarly debates. Public knowledge of the history of German colonialism is subject to a double distortion, which Andreas Eckert and Albert Wirtz pointedly described as "not us, the others too."[7] A similar problem is virulent in the field of migration history. For a long time Germany had no history of migration because migrants, *literally*, were not supposed to exist. Just one decade ago, Germany finally acknowledged her status as an immigration country. Nevertheless, migration is still treated as an exception. In a similar manner, Germany's role in the European colonial project is subject to dismissal or even denial.

The repercussions of this neglect are far reaching. Based on the double denial of both migration and colonial history alike, the Federal Republic of Germany presented the arrival of the one millionth *Gastarbeiter* Armando Rodrigues de Sá 1964 as the beginning of immigration, forcefully suggesting that there has been no migration to Germany prior to this. As a result, historical phenomena such as the presence of Blacks long before the Second World War or the self-organized migration that occurred well before the first official recruitment contracts were signed were erased from historical memory. For the same reasons, German migration policy appeared to be able to successfully control migration at all times. Migration, in turn, seemed to be reducible to socio-economic determinants only, to circumstances beyond the migrants' subjectivities. The history of colonialism remained that of the Global South; just like the reasons of migratory movements to Europe. Due to these patterns in public perception, the idea of Europe emerging from a (post)colonial condition has not found more resonance in public or scholarly debates.

The argument I would like to present here is that migration movements made a significant contribution to the *entangled history* of Europe. They constitutively and repeatedly baulk at incorporation into a community defined in terms of the nation state, and call this into question. The common myth of the unwanted and unintentional settlement of migrants in Europe, implying that the continent's multicultural identity emerged just after the Second World War, suggests a shared European identity that exits despite of the competition and conflicts among the individual nation states. However, this myth also obscures the double transformation of colonial subjects (in terms of citizen-subjects) into "Ausländer" (foreigners) as well as of former migrant workers (e.g. from Portugal, Spain or Italy) into European citizens. In short, this narrative puts the history of colonialism in parentheses.[8]

III. Connecting the History of Colonialism and Migration History: The British Perspective

The relationship between (post)colonialism and migration constitutes one of the key stones of academic research of racism and its history. One among many excellent examples for this approach is the groundbreaking collection *The Empire Strikes Back*, published by the *Birmingham Center for Contemporary Cultural Studies* (CCCS) in 1982. About ten years later, the CCCS author Paul Gilroy coined the metaphor of the Black Atlantic. His publication became the starting point of a larger analysis of the African diaspora and a "black cultural identity," investigating the real as well as the imagined connections Black communities in the United States and Britain shared with African history.[9] In his book, first published in 1993, Gilroy refers to the "middle passage" within the triangular slave trade between Europe, Africa and the New World and reconstructs how different genres of Black music in these regions developed and transformed. Also, he produces a critique of essentialist concepts of race, a topic that will dominate his oeuvre until today.[10]

Gilroy also develops a research design that is in fact crucial for the idea of entangled histories and finds its successors in the critique of methodological nationalism in the context of migration theory and transnational research.[11] About ten years later, in 2005, Gilroy's book *After Empire. Melancholia and Convivial Culture* re-conceptualized the relationship between the local and the global units of analysis. In this study, Gilroy describes a form of imperial amnesia; or to be more precise: Great Britain's inability to remember the history of Empire. Ever since this history became a source of anxiety, shame and confusion, it has been diminished, disputed and – if possible – forgotten.[12] Gilroy also calls this amnesia a "post-colonial melancholia" and attributes two, grave consequences to this phenomenon: First, the British regard "postcolonial people," as he calls them, as "unwanted alien intruders without any substantive historical, political or cultural connection to the collective life of their fellow citizens."[13] Secondly, as Gilroy observes, Great Britain's post-colonial conflicts (such as Palestine, Cyprus, and Ireland) are mysteriously removed from public consciousness.[14]

It seems to be exactly this post-colonial melancholia that spreads all over Europe today. In a time in which connections between the local and the global are more permeable than ever before, the local or the national are increasingly played off against the global rather than being used to reveal the nation as the result of historical power-relationships that are massively transformed today.[15] Instead of putting the history of colonialism into parentheses, we should perhaps begin to put the history of nation states into parentheses.

IV. A Tentative Approach

My project here remains a tentative one for the moment. I will start by collecting several historical accounts (or dispatches) in order to develop a possible frame for connecting postcolonial theory and migration research. These accounts will call upon certain images, however, not as evidence of some form of causality, but as practices capable to insert fissures in traditional historicism. Instead, my argument will explore these fissures, contradictions, and repetitions thereby demonstrating the analytical potential of connecting (post)colonialism and migration. My arrangement of accounts aims at exposing the dissonance between reality and utopia. The accounts themselves provide a tentative access to lived experiences, forcing the reader to study the radical specificities of places and events. All examples I have chosen for this essay discuss migration to Germany, i.e. migration movements to the center of Europe. To focus on Germany is of particular interest here, since this part of European migration history is rather unknown in international debates in contrast to the more popular examples of Great Britain and France. The German case, however, gives me the opportunity to convey an impression of how political engagement of migrants resonated differently in different parts of Europe.

Moreover, it is important to keep in mind that the dispatches chosen here do not fit the spatial logic of (post)colonialism, i.e. they do not fit neatly into one particular nation's empire and its (former) territory. Instead, the accounts document the political activities of migrants. As such, they include transnational interconnections and relationships that constituted and simultaneously decentralized Europe. My selection of discrepant examples may appear as nothing more than an arbitrarily suggested connection. But even as an untheorized compilation of historical incidents, they reveal political contexts which (as I would like to suggest) are relevant for an analysis of the cosmopolitan present and future of Europe. The interconnectedness of political horizons that become apparent by looking at the historical dispatches from a postcolonial perspective, urges us to re-think the concept of progress and its teleology. And there is yet another important aspect to be mentioned: since Europe is presented as a comparatively stable and homogeneous entity today, we have to counterbalance this hegemonic narrative by focusing on processes of impoverishment, on conflicts, and relationships of oppression. We need to take into account the subjective dimension and the acts of solidarity and resistance, which resulted from migration and operated across or even beyond national borders.

In the following analysis, I will differentiate between three different contributions migrants made to such a political entanglement. In the first example, I demonstrate that migrant organizations existed in Europe and in the context of anti-colonial politics long before the end of the Second World War. These organizations actively and critically questioned the concept of European citizenry and belonging. In a second example, I demonstrate how transnational migrant organizations remained intact even during the climax of state nationalism, thereby simultaneously functioning as a forum for anti-capitalist critique. Due to this characteristic, these movements can even be seen as an intellectual predecessor of today's anti-globalization movements. In fact, these movements grew out of the political migrants' political networks. As such, they connect the colonial past and the migrants' present. Referring to a third and last account, my paper will finally illustrate how migration as movement represents the materialist and organized form of such entanglements based on networks and supporters. This illustration will contribute to the exploration of the political potential of different forms of migrant's organizations concerning both their potential to engender social change and their contribution to the constitution of Europe as a postcolonial formation.[16] Moreover, this focus establishes an analytic starting point for future research that aims at retracing and understanding the complex postcolonial conditions of Europe.

V. Dispatch 1: Anti-Colonial Migrants and Civil Rights in Europe[17]

In 1918, a group of colonial migrants founded the *Afrikanischen Hilfsverein* in Hamburg. All of them were initially considered citizens of the German Reich ("Reichsdeutsche") but soon categorized as stateless. Although the association was officially bound to political neutrality, it was instrumental in organizing a diasporic consciousness among migrants from African countries. It publicly protested against the campaign against the "Schwarze Schande" (Black Shame) which was rampaging across Germany between 1923 and 1930, and which was dovetailed by racist assaults on black Germans and their children.[18] The *Hilfsverein* was only one of several organizations founded in this period. In 1926, for instance, the *Liga gegen koloniale Unterdrückung* (League Against

Colonial Oppression) was founded by the *Initiative der Internationalen Arbeiterhilfe* (IAH, Initiative of the International Workers' Association) in cooperation with the communist journalist and Member of the Reichstag Willi Münzenberger. In the following year, the *Liga* participated, as suggested by Münzenberger, in organizing an anti-colonial congress on 10 February 1927 at the Palais Egmont in Brussels. This conference was attended by 174 delegates from all over the world, including Jawaharlal Nehru, Mohammed Hatta, and Albert Einstein. It was during this congress that Lamine Senghor announced the foundation of the Parisian *Ligue de la Défense de la Race Nègre* (League for the Defense of the Negro).

This organization found its counterpart in the German *Liga zur Verteidigung der Negerrasse*, established 1929 in Berlin.[19] Referring to the already existing networks Cameroonian migrants in Berlin, the *Liga* developed an anti-colonial agenda, resulting in a radicalization of German Africans aligned with the Comintern, and established connections to activists in cities across Europe as well as in Cameroon. In 1930, the *Liga* organized the first "Internationale Konferenz der Negerarbeiter" (First International Conference of Negro Workers) in Hamburg, which was attended by delegates from Africa, the United States and the Caribbean. In the same year, also the *International Trade Union Committee of Negro Workers* (ITUCNW) was founded. Serving as the Comintern's union branch, it quickly developed into a global network. The ITUCNW published *The Negro Worker*, a monthly periodical which was edited by the Trinidadian George Padmore and was distributed across the globe by sailors starting out from Hamburg.

Due to the influence of the Soviet Union, the Comintern offered an organizational framework for numerous anti-colonial organizations. In the late 1920s, many of them were located in Berlin. This "involuntary postcoloniality," as Tobias Nagl has phrased it, of the Weimar Republic transformed Berlin into a European "anti-colonial metropole."[20] Connecting anti-colonial efforts to the Comintern, however, often resulted in a highly ambiguous situation. On the one hand, individual Black activists became representatives of racial discrimination suffered by people of African descent worldwide. On the other hand, this cooperation allowed for a critique of white privilege and an acknowledgement of their political expertise. Moreover, these joint efforts promised to overcome not only racist hierarchies, but also traumatizing experiences and memories of violence by establishing a transnational framework for the articulation of common political interests of people from Africa, the United States, and Europe.[21]

All of these activities rested upon the ability to move freely between the colonial metropoles and their respective colonies as well as on the (often only temporary) inclusion of migrants by European citizenship regulations. Both freedom of movement and citizenship rights were the preconditions for establishing an organized political resistance against the (by then) still existent colonial order. In turn, these movements put a thorn in the side of proponents of simplistic and racist notions of European citizenship. It is precisely this dimension of anti-colonial struggles, namely their impact on citizenship rights and concepts of freedom of movement, which I consider a central characteristic of a postcolonial Europe.

VI. Europe's Frontiers and the Transformation of Citizenship

As demonstrated in my first dispatch, migrants in Europe established organizations, networks, and financial structures transcending the narrow perspective of nation states, which call for an analysis from a postcolonial perspective. Achille Mbembe has described such an approach as follows:

> What constitutes the political strength of postcolonial thought is its enrolment in the historic social struggles of colonized societies and especially its rereading of the theoretical praxis of what we call liberation movements. So it is a way of thinking which, in several respects, still believes in the postulate that the only true learning is the learning that aims to transform the world.[22]

In other words, these historical anti-colonial practices allow us to develop new forms of knowledge, which connect to current political conflicts and struggles. A situation to which theoretical thinkers such as Gilroy and Balibar respond by developing concepts such as "conviviality" or "cosmo-politics."[23] Migration movements and their struggles expose the gap between Europe's postcolonial condition and its spatial, temporal, and "latitudinal" distortions.

An analysis of historical and contemporary forms and practices of transnational migrant organizations helps us to understand the transformations of ideas and institutions of citizenship in Europe today. Such transformations have far reaching consequences for the very concept of citizenship. The fact that we are confronted with the emergence and conceptualization of a European citizenship and that this process runs parallel with a re-drawing of European borders, makes the question of citizenship an urgent issue of postcolonial perspectives. From a postcolonial angle, it is not enough to observe institutional change. Rather, we must examine forms of migrant organizations in order to portray them as the agents of the transformation of borders and citizenship. As the first account has shown, the concept of citizenship has been disputed from the very beginning; its borders were shifted in political and social struggles, while the same struggles testify to the capability of migrants to move and to organize. Therefore we need to acknowledge that the nation state has been and is challenged as well as radically transformed by such struggles. For migrants it was inevitable to establish a form of politics that transcended the nation state as a space that is still widely assumed as the proper space of the political. It is this national space that still forms the basis of many scholarly studies and which we need to leave behind in order to fully understand its history.

VII. Dispatch 2: "This Fourth World is the Third World, at our home"[24]

In 1971 – before most of the Western European countries issued their recruitment ban for *Gastarbeiter* (guest workers) – a small but illustrious group of activists brought together by the philosopher Andrè Grosz and the sociologist Charles Bettelheim met in the small Italian town of Tarquinia. They were guests of Roberto Matta, a surrealist painter, sculptor, and architect from Chile. Matta had invited the two Marxist thinkers and a number of other people, some of them with migrational background, from all over Western Europe, to discuss the current "radicalization of class struggles" that he and other Marxists were convinced they were witnessing. Their main and simultaneously provocative thesis was that the "immigrated workers" in Europe were in fact part of the "Fourth World."[25] The participants claimed that their arrival in Europe signaled "the incursion of Third World struggles into the imperial citadel."[26] It is important to note that this gathering was – at least to my knowledge – the only (documented) meeting of scholars and migrants which developed a decidedly European perspective. The broader, European angle manifested in a comparison of the situation of European immigration countries (including Western Germany, Great Britain, France, and Switzerland) and emigration countries (Portugal, Italy, and Algiers). All of them were seen as part of a general development of capitalist relations of production, a point of view that also accounted for imperial and colonial strategies.

To give a more detailed impression of migration organizations during this period, I would like to add another example. In 1969, the *Círculo Cultural* or *Spanisches Zentrum* (Spanish Cultural Center) was founded in Essen.[27] Starting in 1972, the Center organized so-called Spanish weeks on a yearly basis for the next four years to follow. By employing these cultural events, the organizers aimed at addressing two major political points: first, the situation of migrants in Europe and second, the social, political, and economic situation in Spain and in other nation states. The Center's activists invited musicians and authors from Spain, France, Portugal, Italy, Chile, and Uruguay, whose works of art sometimes had been banned in their home countries. The main goal of the Center's activities was to share different experiences of political struggles and to encourage solidarity. The international setup of the Center resulted in a large political network.[28]Activist Rafael Sanchez explained the self-directed organizational form of the Center and emphasized its international character at a celebration at the *Grugahalle* (a large indoor event and sports arena) in Essen. From today's perspective his words resonate with the arguments of an anti-globalization movement that had yet to emerge twenty years later:

> The Spanish Cultural Center is part of a broader autonomist movement, that currently emerges everywhere and at all levels, a movement that we see in Italy, France, Portugal, Chile, Spain, and also in the Federal Republic of Germany, a movement that rejects all forms of bureaucra-

> cy and that will not be guided by any party or group, but that is self-determined and therefore allows for an open debate among those affected [...]. On this way to a collective struggle many additional steps need to be taken, steps of shared dispute, of shared experience, of discussing our experiences made in different fields, because only the concurrence of diverse opinions and experiences facilitates a debate as well as a development that helps us. Maybe, all this sounds like dreams of the future, since we all know how difficult it is to build such associations, but I think that we need to keep this in mind despite all the difficulties and that in fact, here and today, we already have begun to do so, because what we experience here is our collective cause.[29]

In the Center, two typical forms of organization were joined. First, it established, quite literally, a space of communication, where many of the local, national and international political debates of that time circulated and which was connected to a large network of contacts to various countries. Second, it offered room to organize political events and to conduct campaigns. One of the Center's prime concerns was what today would be called anti-racism. It was wanted to provide self-directed structures to immigrant workers to enable them to address their common concerns but not restricted to one national group. This organizational framework helped to oppose racism, by enabling migrants to take action against bad housing conditions and the discrimination against their children in the German educational system. Activists raised public awareness of migrants' civil rights by protesting against deportations and discrimination. Also, they provided guidance and support in legal questions, such as obtaining and upholding permissions of residence.

Secondly, the Center was an integral part of everyday life. The combination of political and cultural activities offered an open structure, including a bookshop, a cinema, or festivals, which were accessible even for those who were not actively involved in political programs. A system of advisory services on health and legal issues as well as language classes, for instance, also supported migrant households on an economic level by relieving their budgets. Thus, the Center established a structure that sustained the reproduction and resistance of migrants and their networks.

Moreover, the Center's activists claimed to establish a global movement that transcended national borders. A claim that was well-grounded as can be seen by looking at the international contacts listed in the address given at the *Grugahalle*. It allows us to catch an initial glimpse of today's political global movement which, at this point, was yet to emerge but relies on the achievements of these early migration movements.

VIII. Globalization: Primitive Accumulation, World Market and the Mobility of Labor

Today, many authors refer to the term 'globalization' to describe the mechanisms and social or political entanglements I have described above. It is, however, important to note that the term 'globalization' differs from the notion of 'postcolonialism' significantly, as the latter explicitly evokes the historical circumstances that created our globalized world in the first place. Globalization is a new version of an old topic: the displacement of labor that Marx describes in his chapter on the "primitive accumulation" in the first volume of *Das Kapital*.[30] Or, as Marx observes in his *Grundrisse*: "The tendency to create the *world market* is directly given in the concept of capital itself. Every limit appears as a barrier to be overcome."[31] Slave trade, colonial wars, fraud contracts and transfers, the limitation and displacement of labor forces are aspects that were, according to him, preconditions for realizing primitive accumulation. Generally speaking, the accumulation of capital reproduces the relationship between capital and labor as its basis. With reference to Marx's definition, I would like to stress three aspects. First, the accumulation of capital is related to a long-standing mutual relationship between colonialism and capitalism. Second, an analysis of the mobility of workers today demonstrates that primitive accumulation remains the basic principle of an ongoing process of capital accumulation. Third, the history of primitive accumulation is an integral part of the history of Europe.[32]

All central elements of primitive accumulation are discernable in present developments, albeit in new forms: the formation of special economic zones, the merciless mismanagement revealed by the so called financial crisis, the changes in conventional communal usage of water supplies, of land and forest, or food resources due to speculation as well as the massive displacement of laborers (called global migration movements). Other examples of these contemporary forms of primitive accumulation are: the division of workers from the means of production through expulsion or forced migration, the inclusion of workers as stake holders of enterprises, and the emergence of 'motivational migration' (Green Card, Blue Card, etc.), and the massive 'destruction' of the labor force. Furthermore, we can observe the establishment of forms of production that deny labor regulations as superfluous as well as the creation of neocolonial and imperial relationships through exploitation, which within national territories sometimes is referred to as 'internal colonialism.' All of these developments affect mostly but not exclusively those workers who, because of their transformation into independent managers of themselves, sell their labor force undocumented and unorganized and therefore can easily be forced to accept any kind of working condition. All of these aspects suggest that we arrived at a new phase of the so-called primitive accumulation.[33]

IX. Dispatch 3: Ships of Solidarity

The same processes become most apparent if we consider the conditions those migrants who tried to enter to the EU in the year in which the so-called Arab Spring blew a new political breeze across the Mediterranean Sea. In this region alone, more than 2000 people died from hunger or thirst during their attempt to migrate to Europe in the first six months of 2011. Thousands were stuck in desert camps such as the Tunisian city Choucha, or in countries disrupted by civil war like Libya.[34] Often, their only hope was a dangerous passage in overcrowded and feckless boat. Simultaneously, these conditions led to the emergence of transnational solidarity networks. Human rights organizations and anti-racist networks began to appeal for the immediate admission of refugees into the EU:

> The voices of Choucha represent the desperate revolt against a policy of flagrant violation of human rights, as they occur every day at many focal points along the external borders of Europe. A clean break with of this policy is essential to put an end to the deaths at Sea and in the desert. The democratic movements in North Africa offer the opportunity for a new beginning. Instead of lethal exclusion and grotesque threat scenarios, openness and solidarity must characterize the future of the Mediterranean region. It takes bridges instead of walls for a new relationship between Africa and Europe, so that Europe will become a space of true freedom, universal security, and equal rights for all.[35]

The initiative *Ships of Solidarity* called for a general official admission of asylum seekers by European governments. This appeal was articulated at a time, when more and more survivors testified that border patrols deliberately refused to help refugees on overcrowded and leaking boats, tacitly accepting the refugees' eventual death. Simultaneously, the European Union sponsored flights for Sub-Saharan migrants in Tunisia, whose return to their home countries further destabilized their countries' economic situation.

The political uprisings of North Africa also challenged existing contracts between EU and North African countries that were designed to seal off the Southern European borders according to anti-migration EU policies. Accordingly, the EU pressured the (interim) governments to patrol their coast lines, and to cooperate with the *European Union Agency for Border Security, Frontex*. If these demands were not met, the EU threatened to exert economic sanctions. In early 2011, Tunisia hosted about 500.000 refugees from Libya. It was in this situation that a number of European and African organizations established a new network *Afrique-Europe-Interact*, to launch a counter-campaign called *Ships of Solidarity*. Currently, they plan to rent several ships whose mission, starting in April 2012, will be to ensure that refugees at sea will be given necessary assistance. In addition, the activists appeal to EU institutions and governments on both sides of the Mediterranean Sea to establish relationships based on mutual exchange and reciprocity. The Ships will have political personalities, journalists, artists and representatives of the project's partner organizations on board.[36]

X. The Power of Migration

As this third account illustrates, immigration rarely occurs without networks. These in turn emerge either in the course of migration movements or establish themselves to benefit from these activities – a phenomenon that has been the subject of many anthropological studies on transnationalism in recent years. As we know from this research, the migration of laborers to the Federal Republic of Germany during the 1950s also relied on such networks. These findings challenge the hitherto predominant assumption that post-war immigration has been fully regulated by recruitment policies of the German nation state. It is important to note, however, that these forms of self-organization occurred under conditions that differ significantly from those of today in terms of communication and transport:[37]

Next to official recruitment commissions, private agencies played an important role. They organized, at times even on a large scale, the entry of hundreds of migrants as tourists, utilized community structures of the migrants' home villages, and worked on both paid as well as voluntary basis. From time to time, these agencies operated as a facilitator of the migrant's home country, for instance at his or her place of arrival or places of everyday life such as train stations, job centers and cafés. Sometimes, these agencies were commissioned by enterprises and employers. Most of all, these private agencies covered emigration countries for which the Federal Republic had scheduled only small or no immigration contingents. They facilitated or accelerated procedures of immigration. Their main function was to gather and distribute a range of information. Such information includes their destination, travel arrangements and names of contact persons, information about potential employees, cities or regions interested in foreign workers, housing opportunities, and how to acquire immigration documents and residence permits legally and illegally.

It was general knowledge that undocumented entries had been legalized ex post by several alien departments of the Federal Republic and many individual and collective immigration strategies relied on this possibility. The widespread practice of organizing immigration beyond the control of the state, in turn, influenced negotiations on official recruitment arrangements. In 1962, for instance, Morocco refused to prohibit private agencies as long as Moroccan citizens currently living in the Federal Republic had not been granted residence permits. Moreover, Morocco demanded a guarantee that Moroccans would be allowed to enter legally.[38] This situation is comparable to the position Europe's neighbors find themselves in today. On the one hand they are forced to serve as buffer zones and collaborators of European migration policies. On the other hand, enabled by the 'power of migration,' they can defend their own interests by blackmailing the EU.

Generally speaking, the mobility of the labor force certainly must be understood as a vital component of any form of primitive accumulation and thus as a source of exploitation wherever capitalism relies on this flexibility. Yet, mobility also facilitates – as demonstrated by the above-mentioned examples of solidarity and organization – an escape from existing conditions of exploitation and oppression.

XI. Connecting the Dots: Yesterday, Today, Tomorrow

To summarize, entanglements are not only of concern from a historical perspective, as phenomena of the past, but also – as we learn from Gilroy's observation on postcolonial melancholia – of the present. This observation urges us to conceptualize migration as a constituent part of post-war Europe along with the European colonial project. Or, to phrase it differently, we have to account for the fact that both, Europe and its 'Others,' emerged as entities from their respective postcolonial conditions. Bearing these considerations in mind, it does not come as a surprise that the few existing studies on the relationship between migration and postcolonialism focus the questions of racism and citizenship. There is, after all, a strongly structural resemblance between the manner Europe treats its migrants today and the way colonial rule produced privileged citizens and unprivileged subjects. Colonial rule continues in this form of differentiation by translating it into the category of class: While today migrant elites all over Europe have emancipated themselves by acquiring citizenship rights, the same rights are considered provisory for others. The creation of 'migrants,' 'races,' and 'ethnicities' was underpinned and reproduced by colonial institutions. Since we often look for agency only in relationship to institutions, we neglect to study it in a historical perspective. By doing so, we could reconstruct the extent to which colonial institutions determined the agency of colonized and migrants alike. Consequently, we should focus on the formation of identities by the state, how identities are being inscribed into laws and how they are asserted by the law. Ultimately, these identities inform our relationship to the state and to each other.

Using the metaphor of entanglement to describe Europe's postcolonial condition, however, should not invoke the notion of a linear course of time and a smooth and homogenous space. Rather, I would like to suggest that we follow the argument of the anthropologist Aihwa Ong, who developed the concept of latitudinal spaces. While new transnational, social and overlapping spaces emerge, clear 'affiliations' are increasingly often questioned or even dissolved.[39] Ong's considerations can be applied to contemporary Europe. They implicate how the dangerous attempt to externalize Europe's colonial past and to separate postcolonialism and migration already have inscribed itself into concepts of European identity that have come to constitute this very Europe.

Yet, externalization is an ambiguous process. As Europe's border regimes and its democratic processes demonstrate, it is impossible to separate immigration patterns from the actual presence and the participation of the migrants themselves. Clearly, it is also impossible to 'manage' them unilaterally. It is this interconnectedness between postcolonial, political, and theoretical thought on migration that ultimately will bring about the decolonization of Europe.

Notes:

[1] "Der ausländische Arbeiter ist der europäische Bürger von morgen. Der europäische Arbeiter geht dem europäischen Bürger voran." KB/Hamburg, "Westdeutsche Arbeiter – ausländische Arbeiter – eine Arbeiterklasse," Arbeiterkampf 30 (1973): 6-7.

[2] Étienne Balibar, We, the People of Europe? Reflections on Transnational Citizenship (Princeton: Princeton University Press, 2004), 177. The notion of a citizenship in Europe is addressed by Balibar in order to distinguish it from a "European citizenship." By doing so he is opening up the possibility for a citizenship for immigrants that moves conceptually beyond the historical relation between territory and population.

[3] The German "Gastarbeiter" stresses the preliminary status of immigrants as temporary workers, hence the euphemistic term 'guests' i.e. workers who were supposed to leave the country at the end of their contracts.

[4] Balibar, We, the People of Europe, 38-42.

[5] Among many others: Étienne Balibar, "Europe, an 'Unimagined' Frontier of Democracy," diacritics 33,3-4 (2003): 36-44; Prem Poddar, Rajeev S. Patke and Lars Jensen, A Historical Companion to Postcolonial Literatures. Continental Europe and its Empires (Edinburgh: Edinburgh University Press, 2011).

[6] Sebastian Conrad and Shalini Randeria, "Geteilte Geschichten – Europa in einer postkolonialen Welt," in Jenseits des Eurozentrismus. Postkoloniale Perspektiven in den Geschichts- und Kulturwissenschaften, eds. eid. (Frankfurt am Main: Campus, 2002), 9-49. Randeria introduced the concept of entangled histories in the context of a larger debate on the constitution of modernity within and through colonialism. In particular, she pushed for critical reflections on the notion of multiple, respectively plural modernities. Shalini Randeria, "Entangled Histories of Uneven Modernities. Civil Society, Caste Solidarities and Legal Pluralism in Post-Colonial India," in Unraveling Ties. From Social Cohesion to New Practices of Connectedness, eds. Yehuda Elkana et al. (Frankfurt am Main: Campus, 2002), 284-311.

[7] Andreas Eckert and Albert Wirz, "Wir nicht, die anderen auch," in Jenseits des Eurozentrismus, eds. Sebastian Conrad and Shalini Randeria, 372-92.

[8] See Sandrine Berteaux, "The Mediterranean Sea in the Age of the European Union. Postcolonial Politics and Migration Management." Paper presented at

the conference “Migration and Borderlands: Dynamics of Exclusion and Inclusion,” Istanbul, 14-16 April 2011.

9 Paul Gilroy, The Black Atlantic (London: Verso, 1993).

10 Ibid., see most notably Chapter 3.

11 Linda Basch, Nina Glick-Schiller and Christina Szanton Blanc, Nations Unbound. Transnational Projects, Postcolonial Predicaments, and Deterritorialized Nation-States (Basel: Gordon and Breach, 1995). Markus Redicker's and Peter Linebaug's recent work The Many-Headed Hydra. The Hidden History of the Revolutionary Atlantic (Boston: Beacon Press, 2000) is one example of such a conceptually broadened frame that ascribes to the field of Global Labour History.

12 Paul Gilroy, Postcolonial Melancholia (New York: Columbia University Press, 2005), 90.

13 Ibid.

14 Ibid., 89.

15 Graham McPhee and Prem Poddar, “Nationalism beyond the Nation-State,” in Empire and After. Englishness in Postcolonial Perspective, eds. eid (New York and Oxford: Berghahn, 2007), 4.

16 Although this text cannot discuss the different forms of migrants' organizing in detail, it is nevertheless important to note the distinction between forms of migrant self-organization and institutional-oriented forms of organization. This differentiation is significant because the respective form of organization came along with varying requirements for members and addressed varying political recipients, which altogether involved varying ideas of the political (with regard to space and influence).

17 A wonderful and rather unknown insight into political activities of anti-colonial migrants in Germany is given by Tobias Nagel in his book Die unheimliche Maschine. Rassismus und Repräsentation im Weimarer Kino (München: edition text + kritik, 2009). I rely on his work in my first account, which focuses on the years of Weimar Republic; a period that preceded the repression of migrant politics under NS rule. The book offers an interesting overview about transnational connections between European Blacks and the political, cultural and intellectual communities of Afro-America. In addition, I refer to the paper “Colonial Migration and Metropolitan Anti-Colonialism” held by Nathanael Kuck in 2011 at the conference “Migration, Mobility and Movement in Modern German History,” University of Cambridge, Faculty of History, 29-31 March 2011.

18 Starting in Germany, the “black shame” campaign assumed international outreach and reached its climax in the 1920s. The campaign discredited the French troops from colonial Africa in the occupation of Rhineland. The campaign made use of mutually supportive sexist, nationalist, anti-Semitic and racist ideologies. Tina M. Campt, Other Germans. Black Germans and the Politics of Race, Gender and Memory in the Third Reich (Ann Arbor, Mich.: Uni-

versity of Michigan Press, 2004); Fatima El-Tayeb, "Dangerous Liaisons. Race, Nation, and German Identity," in Not so Plain as Black and White. Afro-German Culture and History 1890-2000, eds. Patricia Mazón and Reinhild Steingröver (Rochester: University of Rochester Press, 2005), 27-60; Iris Wigger, Die "Schwarze Schmach am Rhein". Rassistische Diskriminierung zwischen Geschlecht, Klasse, Nation und Rasse (Münster: Westfälisches Dampfboot, 2007).

[19] Among the founding members were the Cameroonian architect Joseph Ekwe Bidé and the actor Louis Brody. See also Robbie Aitken, "From Cameroon to Germany and Back via Moscow and Paris. The Political Career of Joseph Bilé (1892-1959), Performer, 'Negerarbeiter' and Comintern Activist," Journal of Contemporary History 43 (2008): 597-616. The foundation was initiated by a short visit of Tiémoko Garan Kouyatés, a member of the "Ligue de la Défense de la Race Nègre," to Willi Münzenberger.

[20] Nagl, Die unheimliche Maschine, 620.

[21] Ibid., 632.

[22] Achille Mbembe, "What is Postcolonial Thinking? An Interview with Achille Mbembe," http://www.eurozine.com/articles/2008-01-09-mbembe-en.html (accessed 21 Oct. 2012), 3.

[23] Gilroy, The Black Atlantic; Étienne Balibar, "Strangers as Enemies. Further Reflections on the Aporias of Transnational Citizenship. Globalization Working Papers 06/4 of the Institute on Globalization and the Human Condition," http://www.socialsciences.mcmaster.ca/institute-on-globalization-and-the-human-condition/publications-1/working-papers-series-1/browse-titles (accessed 21 Oct. 2012), 9.

[24] Daniel Anselme, Charles Bettelheim et al., Die Fremdarbeiter. Die Radikalisierung der Klassenkämpfe durch die "Vierte Welt". Beiträge von der Arbeitsbesprechung in Tarquinia 1971 (Gaiganz: Politladen Erlangen, 1974), 12.

[25] Ibid.

[26] Ibid., 9.

[27] In its self-portrayal the Center described itself as a role model for the self-organization of workers, emerging from the necessity of foreign workers to address their problems directly and on their own terms. Since both German and Spanish institutions alike were unable to respond to migrants' problems adequately, self-organization seemed a logical consequence for doing politics. To quote from the German original: "Das Spanische Kulturzentrum in Essen ist ein Modell einer Arbeiter-Selbstorganisation, entstanden aus der dringenden Notwendigkeit der ausländischen Arbeiter, ihre Probleme selbst in die Hand zu nehmen, sowie als logische Konsequenz der absoluten Unfähigkeit deutscher sowie spanischer Institutionen, unsere Probleme zu beantworten." Cited from Spanisches Zentrum Essen, Spanien ist anders (München: Trikont, 1975), 5.

[28] Informations-Dienst zur Verbreitung unterbliebener Nachrichten Nr. 109, 1976.

[29] "Der Spanische Kulturkreis ist ein Teil einer breiten autonomen Bewegung, die heute überall auf allen Ebenen entsteht, einer Bewegung, die wir in Italien, Frankreich, Portugal, Chile, Spanien und auch in der BRD erleben, einer Bewegung, die alle bürokratischen Formen ablehnt und sich von keiner Partei oder Gruppe führen läßt, sondern sich selbst bestimmt und deshalb eine offene Auseinandersetzung unter den Betroffenen ermöglicht. [...] Auf diesem Weg zu einem gemeinsamen Kampf sind noch sehr viele Schritte notwendig, Schritte der gemeinsamen Auseinandersetzung, der gemeinsamen Erfahrung, der Diskussion unserer Erfahrungen aus den verschiedenen Bereichen, weil nur das Zusammentreffen vieler verschiedener Meinungen und Erfahrungen die Diskussion ermöglicht sowie eine Entwicklung, die uns weiterbringt. Vielleicht klingt das alles noch wie Zukunftsmusik, weil wir alle wissen, wie schwer es ist, solche Zusammenhänge aufzubauen, ich meine aber, daß wir trotz aller Schwierigkeiten diese Sache im Kopf behalten müssen und im Grunde schon heute damit angefangen haben, denn was wir hier zusammen erleben, ist unsere gemeinsame Sache." Cited from the Album Leben. Kämpfen. Solidarisieren, Essen, Grugahalle, 27 November 1976.

[30] In original: "so genannten ursprünglichen Akkumulation" and "Die Tendenz, den Weltmarkt zu schaffen, ist unmittelbar im Begriff des Kapitals selbst gegeben. Jede Grenze erscheint als zu überwindende Schranke."

[31] Karl Marx, Grundrisse. Outlines of the Critique of Political Economy (London: Penguin, 1973 [1857-1861], 410, emphasis in the original.

[32] We can make similar observations about the gender dimension of the history of capitalism. In her feminist analysis of the processes of primitive accumulation, Silvia Federici focuses on witch-hunts of the sixteenth and seventeenth centuries. She states: "[T]he persecution of the witches in Europe as in the New World, was as important as colonization and the expropriation of the European peasantry from its land were for the development of capitalism." Silvia Federici, "The Great Caliban. The Struggle Against the Rebel Body," The Commoner 3 (2002), http://www.commoner.org.uk/03federici.pdf (accessed 21 Oct. 2012). Thus, her analysis transcends the traditional feminist interpretation of witch-hunts as the destruction of female control over biological reproduction. She offers a perspective that re-aligns the classical division of class and gender from a specific historical perspective, by demonstrating how women became constitutive elements in class struggles.

[33] Ranabir Samaddar, "Primitive Accumulation and Some Aspects of Work and Life in India," Economic and Political Weekly XLIV,18 (2009): 33-42.

[34] Choucha is a UNHCR refugee camp in Tunisia close to the Libyan border. See http://www.medico.de/themen/menschenrechte/migration/dokumente/choucha-appell/4021/ (accessed 21 Oct. 2012).

[35] Translated from "Appell" June 2011, http://www.afrique-europe-interact.net/index.php?article_id=544&clang=0 (accessed 21 Oct. 2012).

[36] Ibid.

[37] Ludger Pries, Die Transnationalisierung der sozialen Welt. Sozialräume jenseits von Nationalgesellschaften (Frankfurt am Main: Suhrkamp, 2008), 49.
[38] Manuela Bojadžijev, Die windige Internationale. Rassismus und Kämpfe der Migration (Münster: Westfälisches Dampfboot, 2008); Serhat Karakayali, Gespenster der Migration. Zur Genealogie illegaler Einwanderung in der Bundesrepublik Deutschland (Bielefeld: transcript, 2008).
[39] Aihwa Ong, Neoliberalism as Exception. Mutations in Citizenship and Sovereignity (Durham: Duke University Press, 2006).

Humanitarianism in Postcolonial Contexts: Some West European Examples from the 1960s to the 1980s

Lora Wildenthal

If you want to do something like we did with "A Ship for Vietnam," stay away from the Responsible Officials and the Experts. Governments will not help [...] Governments don't care if people die or are forced to migrate.
(Rupert Neudeck)

In 2009 Rupert Neudeck offered public reflections on the past thirty years of *Cap Anamur*, the humanitarian NGO he helped to found in 1979 that was at first called *A Ship for Vietnam* (*Ein Schiff für Vietnam*).[1] Although he is best known for creating that organization, he did not want his listeners to focus on it as an organization: "In the beginning was not the erection of a bureaucratic structure, in the beginning was just the deed [...] the pure deed."[2] Once word got out to the West German public about *A Ship for Vietnam* through a television announcer's unscheduled statement, donations poured in. His organization was inspired by the 1978 effort of the *Médecins sans Frontières* to send "un bateau pour le Viêt-Nam" to rescue the "boat people" in the South China Sea. The *Médecins sans Frontières'* ship was named *Ile de Lumière*, and their initiative soon became the humanitarian organization *Médecins du Monde* (Doctors of the World), a splinter group of the older organization *Médecins sans Frontières* (Doctors Without Borders).[3] Neudeck's group's ship was named *Cap Anamur*, which soon became the name of the West German organization. In his thirtieth-anniversary remarks, Neudeck emphasized that individual persons responding to the dire need of fellow human beings could accomplish much more than states could.[4]

States appeared in his comments as, at worst, killers of their own people (Neudeck mentioned Zimbabwe here) and, at best, as bureaucratic obstructions. Back in 1979, the West German state had offered no assistance to *A Ship for Vietnam*. On the contrary, civil servants lectured him about how unwise it would be to proceed without retaining legal counsel or taking out insurance. Neudeck stressed that it was essential to ignore such advice.[5] If one worried too much about rules, or about what one did not know, one would hesitate or even abandon one's effort to aid those suffering or even facing imminent death. Neudeck has often cited the character Dr. Rieux from Albert Camus's novel *The Plague*: "'A man can't cure and know at the same time. So let's cure as quickly as we can. That is the most urgent job.'"[6] *Cap Anamur* went on to work in Somalia, Uganda, Ethiopia, Angola, Rwanda, and Sudan, among other African countries, as well as in Bosnia, Kosovo, and Afghanistan (during both the Soviet and US invasions). In those countries, Neudeck emphasized in his remarks, *Cap Anamur* avoided dealing with the state as much as possible, choosing instead partners from local groups such as churches. Of course, the organization continually ran up against barriers erected by states. Fortunately, he noted, international law was coming to recognize the imperatives he and other humanitarians saw, and was moving toward dismissing procedural violations regarding state sovereignty if the clear goal was to aid victims.[7] Indeed, a few months after his remarks, some *Cap Anamur* members were acquitted by an Italian court of a charge of aiding illegal immigration for having rescued Africans stranded in the Mediterranean.[8]

Even such a brief sketch of humanitarian work in our era indicates the institutional and political, as well as logistical, challenges that someone like Rupert Neudeck has faced. Such humanitarians defy states and other powerful institutions; they forge powerful yet evanescent bonds with their donor publics through the media; they carry out actions requiring great personal bravery and endurance; and they rely on cooperation from local people at the sites of humanitarian crisis. They have come to know the political and ethical dilemmas of their work all too well, but they forge ahead, some with, some without state assistance. As Neudeck's quotation from Camus indicates, the point for him is not to contextualize humanitarian disasters in history and politics, but to act. For him, knowledge is paralyzing. Or such was his striking public claim. In fact, Neudeck has a tremendous amount of knowledge about the politics and economics of African countries, which was on display in his remarks; moreover, he stressed that everyone needed to learn much more about the qualitatively new nature of what he called the "wandering of the peoples" (*Völkerwanderung*) now underway in Africa. It was not, he said, enough to throw money at the problem. Yet knowledge did not appear in his public comments as a motivator to action. Instead, decontextualized ethical imperatives did: part of a strategy of self-presentation that implied directness, moral clarity, and the undiluted moral deed.

Scholars and public intellectuals have contextualized humanitarian work in various ways.[9] Critical social scientists have noted the phenomenal growth of the humanitarian sector and highlighted its political and ethical dilemmas. They show that humanitarianism has always been shaped by state action, and has always had a political dimension, even when, as in the 1970s, it was most loudly proclaiming its non-political nature. The development of modern militaries, the Cold War, the "antitotalitarian moment" of the 1970s,[10] and the "war on terror," all have shaped the humanitarianisms as we know them today. These scholars' critical voices, usually from the social sciences, are aimed at reinventing humanitarianism in light of current needs.

The goal of this essay is a different one. Unlike those social scientists, as a historian I have inadequate analytical tools for measuring the intentions and outcomes of these humanitarian endeavors. I do seek to historicize the humanitarians. While that historicization is vital to understanding, I do not presume that historicization invalidates the stated goals of the historical actors, and I have no suggestions for reform. This essay is motivated by the question of the extent to which humanitarians' statements are fruitful texts for grasping popular understandings of sovereignty, race, and power in the world after the Second World War and after the proliferation of new states in the wake of decolonization. Race, the most important "rule of colonial difference," was reconfigured in this era.[11] And so was the states' sovereignty: at the same time that the number of independent states was multiplying, their sovereignty was undergoing a profound challenge. Even as the United Nations enshrined a state-based view of the world in its very structure, its ban on aggressive war and its goal of entangling sovereign states in many kinds of treaties, including those on human rights and humanitarianism, have put pressure on state sovereignty.[12] Humanitarians provide an interesting perspective on the supposedly postcolonial world because they have navigated among old and new states, making use of international law's challenges to sovereignty when they could, and summoning up their own constituencies through new fundraising and public relations campaigns in wealthy states.[13] With regard to race and rights, they have challenged the maxims of both colonialists and Third Worldist anticolonialists. Unlike most in the First World, they have also interacted closely with Africans and Asians in newly independent states. These Africans and Asians have ranged from state officials to fellow medical and other care providers, to the most destitute and desperate. What do humanitarians have to say about the world in which they move, and which they have helped to create?

There is one episode, well-known in the history of humanitarianism, that drew together these strands of sovereignty, race, and human rights. Over the 1960s, Third Worldism took hold on the Left in Europe. That is, activists and intellectuals turned to the newly independent states of the so-called Third World for revolutionary inspiration, in the wake of the collapsing symbolic power of the Soviet Union. In the 1970s, some Leftists in France launched a vehement critique against *tiersmondisme*, rejecting the justification of violence in the name of revolutionary or development projects. They pointed to post-colonial states' violence toward their own citizens as well as toward other states. The case of Vietnam exemplified their critique. Only a few years before, many parts of the Left had denounced US imperialism in Vietnam, and many supported the victory of the North Vietnamese. But in the aftermath of that war, the world was confronted with the Vietnamese 'boat people,' tens of thousands of suffering and dying refugees seeking to escape communist Vietnam. The Third Worldist project paled in light of this suffering. Disillusioned Third Worldists now pointed to non-political criteria for where to direct one's solidarity. In other words, they claimed to drop ideology and politics, a maneuver that extended back to the existentialists, especially Albert Camus and Jean-Paul Sartre. A concomitant effect, as comparative literature scholar Kristin Ross has pointed out, was a shift from seeing people in the Third World as militant actors to passive victims of human rights violations.[14]

Below are brief discussions of some statements from four individuals connected to three humanitarian initiatives from the postwar era and post-decolonization moment. All of them have been highly articulate creators of their own record, as well as effective organizers. The first, Edmond Kaiser, is best known as the founder of the Swiss organization *Terre des Hommes* in 1960, which has aided children affected by war, poverty, disease, and sexual exploitation. The second and third individuals are Cheryl Benard and Edit Schlaffer, two Austrian feminists who founded *Amnesty for Women* in 1981, primarily to aid Afghan women in Pakistani refugee camps. The fourth individual to be discussed here is, again, Rupert Neudeck. Benard and Schlaffer echo the polemics of the *anti-tiersmondisme* debate, and Neudeck was directly inspired by André Glucksmann, Jean-Paul Sartre, Bernard Kouchner, and others close to the *Médecins sans Frontières*.[15] In each of these brief discussions, I have sought to foreground these humanitarians' notions of race and sovereignty.

I. Edmond Kaiser, *Terre des Hommes*, and *Sentinelles*

Edmond Kaiser (1914-2000) was an artist of the anti-ideological statement. He was strongly affected by his experiences of Nazism and the Second World War, decolonization, and the Cold War. Born in Paris to a Jewish family, he lived in Switzerland in his youth. In 1941, his young son died in a household accident, about which he wrote in fictionalized form. During the war he returned to Paris to work in the Resistance, and was condemned to death by the Nazis. After the war was over, he was falsely imprisoned as a traitor. In 1948 he moved back to Lausanne permanently. He worked as a journalist and in business (in earlier years for Philips, and later as pharmaceuticals salesman).[16] Kaiser's response to the Second World War, later political events, and his personal tragedy was an intense impatience with ideologies. Compassion was Kaiser's self-consciously post-ideological commitment. For Kaiser, compassion was the very essence of being human. One expressed compassion not only for the sake of the sufferer, but for one's own sake as well.

Kaiser's idea of compassion drew upon the French author Antoine de St. Exupéry, whom he greatly admired. In the books *Le Petit Prince* and *Terre des Hommes*, St. Exupéry wrote about unselfishness and empathy as the only way to remain human in a world of profound solitude. The very names of Kaiser's organizations were references to St. Exupéry.[17] Perhaps Kaiser's own near-death experiences under Nazism and after its defeat drew him to St. Exupéry, who wrote famously of his own near-death experience of being stranded after an airplane crash in the Saharan desert. Kaiser was also inspired by Albert Camus (as was Neudeck, as we have seen). From Camus's *Myth of Sisyphus* Kaiser drew the following quote and made it a book's epigraph:

> There is only one useful action: that which refers to man on earth. I never refer to men. [...] flesh is my only certainty. I can only live as flesh. The living being is my country.[18]

Camus situated his existentialist tales of moral choice in a pared-down version of colonial Algeria.[19] St. Exupéry placed the Little Prince and his narrator-friend in an even more pared-down Algerian space: the Saharan desert, the site of his own near-death experience. The Little Prince was, of course, from another planet, and Kaiser was obviously inspired by the idea of examining the absurdities and injustices of human interaction on earth from the perspective of a visitor from another planet.

Kaiser, like Neudeck, was impatient with states and with their intergovernmental organizations such as the United Nations. Kaiser was scathing in his communications when polite efforts proved fruitless. In 1980, for example, after years of work on the issues of female genital mutilation and honor violence, he wrote to an official in the Division of Human Rights at the UN:

> We appeal to you, master over life and death, together with [Division of Human Rights Director] Theo van Boven of the tied hands (as he says), we ask you to advise us immediately and in detail, what one can do about the terrorism, silence, incompetence, indifference, the laziness and stupidity of the higher levels of the United Nations Organization.[20]

The *World Health Organization* (WHO) was another target for him. When it finally announced a conference on "traditional practices affecting the health of women and children" (the 1979 Khartoum conference, at which it first addressed female genital cutting), Kaiser described WHO as an awful bird: "Brooding comfortably atop the facts of sexual mutilations inflicted on girls generation after generation, the World Health Organization has now been compelled to leave its rotten nest, which it has occupied for twenty years without saying a word."[21]

Kaiser was similarly impatient with postcolonial governments, which had an ever louder voice at the UN. He found the leaders of these newly independent states to be excessively interested in the trappings of sovereignty, and he delighted in using their attachment to ceremonial etiquette to force them to hear him out. Meeting personally several Third World leaders, he left them spluttering at his calm demands. For an interviewer, he described his techniques of confrontation:

> If I want to see a head of state on the matter of sexual mutilations that are perpetrated in his country, I begin by sending him a fax or telex pointing out (this is not made up, this is real) that I have received two thousand personal letters protesting against female genital mutilation. I add: 'It is I who have received them, but it is you whom they concern; you, who are the head of this state, the father of the poor victims,' etc. I am extremely courteous at this stage. I ask to meet the head of state, in order to give him the letters and talk to him about the problem. The guy usually does not answer. Then I write back two or three weeks lat-

> er in order to confirm that which I had informed him of earlier, reminding him: 'I still have my two thousand letters, they are at your disposal.' After two weeks, I send him a last message that says: 'I have the pleasure to inform you that I will arrive at the airport on such and such a day, by such and such a flight, at such and such an hour; you will be kind enough to have someone fetch me from the airport and bring me to you.' Usually the fellow is so annoyed that it works... Annoyed to the point where one of them sends the ambassador to me in Lausanne to dissuade me. Here is an example of the [French comic] Fernand Raynaud-style dialogue with the ambassador: 'Mr. President Houphouët-Boigny has sent me to ask you not to come.' Me: 'Good, I am coming.' Him: 'I insist, President Houphouët-Boigny requests that you not approach him.' Me: 'Good, then I'm coming.' And so on. And finally you arrive at the time you have chosen, and you are received by two guys who follow diplomatic protocol, but who are perhaps police spies or espionage police, it doesn't matter, and these two henchmen take you exactly where you want to go. Without the least complication. You do not know the head of state, the head of state does not know you, you annoy him, but you reach your goal, and you go from annoyer to guest of state.[22]

Kaiser here has described how simple but persistent attempts at normal communication can breach the bureaucratic and ceremonial stonewalling of a newly independent state (here, Ivory Coast). Apparently, the embarrassment of having this lone European continue to seek an audience persuaded the president's office to get the encounter over with.

Kaiser was also impatient with humanitarian bureaucracies – even his own. He believed that professional humanitarians in large organizations were often more focused on successful careers for themselves than they were on the people they were supposed to help, and that they too easily came to enjoy lording their wealth over the impoverished people who worked for them. Kaiser also held that established humanitarian organizations used criteria for the selection of aid recipients that reflected the organization's need to record successes more than the actual human need. In other words, such humanitarian bureaucracies helped not those who suffered the most, but rather those who were likeliest to recover and flourish.[23] Kaiser's goal was to see through social and political conventions in order to perceive the most despised, helpless, and ignored among the suffering. In the 1950s, this quest had led him to work with the Emmaus movement, founded in 1949 by Abbé Pierre, France's famed advocate of refugees and the homeless.[24] In 1960, the plight of ill and injured Algerian children in the midst of the war came to his attention. He founded *Terre des Hommes*, and faced opposition both from Algerian nationalists and from French who considered him an FLN agent. In its first five years, *Terre des Hommes* aided children from Algeria, Brazil, Ivory Coast, Spain, France,

Greece, Italy, India, Madagascar, Portugal, Senegal, Switzerland, Togo, and Tunisia, a list clearly intended to blur the distinctions between the First and Third Worlds.[25] In the 1970s Kaiser became aware of female genital cutting and 'honor' violence, which led him to cooperate with French feminist Benoïte Groult among others.[26] Girls affected by genital cutting, Kaiser believed, were exactly the kind of sufferers who fell outside the criteria of humanitarian organizations, as well as outside the criteria of human rights organizations (*Amnesty International*, he commented sarcastically, did not consider female genital mutilation to be "la bonne torture").[27] Increasingly frustrated by the reluctance of states, the UN, and even NGOs, including *Terre des Hommes*, to give female genital mutilation highest priority, he severed all ties with *Terre des Hommes* and founded *Sentinelles* in 1980. *Sentinelles* has aided women and children facing genital cutting, honor violence, sexual violence, child marriage, and noma, a disfiguring disease affecting small children.[28]

People outside of the structures of states, the UN, or humanitarian organizations, Kaiser found, were open to unencumbered human interaction. Whether raising money or making the necessary contacts to reach sufferers, Kaiser insisted (as did Neudeck) that it was really all very simple. Kaiser described his formula for spontaneously locating children needing help:

> That happens just as simply [as meeting a head of state]. Once I arrived unexpectedly, by plane, on a landing strip in the north of South Vietnam, during the war. I obviously did not know anyone. So you arrive, and since you know no one and you must, all the same, leave the airport or the landing strip, you go down the road and you reach a village. In the village there is a street, with people eating along it. You talk to them. They look at you with a kind smile and kind eyes, as the Vietnamese are capable of looking at a stranger who introduces himself into their midst during the war, and you tell them, 'I belong to a movement called *Terre des hommes* (as was then the case), and this is what we are trying to do: to help Vietnamese children burned or injured by napalm or otherwise. Would you have any useful contacts?' The people are sometimes upset, sometimes not, and answer you, 'Oh yes? Uh, yes, I do.' They take you to some high functionary, it does not matter which one, a school headmaster, teacher, or nurse of some hospital, it does not matter which, and it is done. Nothing more is necessary.
>
> [Interviewer:] Trust immediately appears?
>
> Yes. At the hospital in Danang, for example, on a bench, there was a woman, one of several, because there were a lot of women like her, with her injured little girl, who suddenly gave me her child, saying 'Bac-si,' which means doctor, 'Bac-si, take her home with you to give her a better life.' In that instance, the contact was not borne of any

> journalistic information I had read, but simply from a different form of encounter. The world is open.[29]

The scene is horrifying: a woman is so desperate that she wishes to give her child to a European stranger on the spur of the moment. Yet Kaiser narrated it as an unmediated gesture of trust and understanding. He transported many hundreds of children to various European destinations in the 1960s. Many of these children were placed in adoptive homes (whether temporary or permanent is unclear). He himself adopted a Senegalese boy, Amadou, who was handicapped due to severe maltreatment. International adoption across racial lines was one of Kaiser's lasting causes, and it was yet another of *Sentinelles'* areas of work. His message to his readers was that it posed no difficulties whatever in actual practice. Onlookers did raise objections: Algerian nationalists who did not want to allow ill children to leave the country, and claimed that Islam forbade adoption; Swiss officials who insisted that an African child could not flourish in Switzerland. Kaiser's point was that uninvolved onlookers conjured up obstacles that did not exist; those who were directly involved did not in fact experience those obstacles.[30] Neudeck made similar points about the integration of Vietnamese refugees into West German society.[31]

In Kaiser's narration, it was the children's home countries that were inhospitable, and Europe that was open and welcoming. Certainly the predicaments of the outcast children and women Kaiser sought to help focused his attention on the hierarchies within postcolonial societies. He sought out not only those suffering from illness and war-related injuries, but also those scorned and maltreated by their fellow nationals, such as the children of prostitutes, and children forced to serve as guides to the blind or to marabouts. Kaiser sought to give such women and children a new home, in a Europe that would not treat them as outcasts. In later years, as *Terre des Hommes* grew, it offered more aid services in the children's home countries, but Kaiser remained convinced of the importance of exiting one's social context through intercontinental travel as a solution.

As much as Kaiser sought to downplay racism and racial difference, it was of course all around him. Indeed, complex political issues lay not far under the surface of his call to respond to immediate (i.e. unpolitical, unhistorical) human suffering by removing a child to Europe. The issue of female genital cutting gained traction in France partly because the French feminist movement seized upon it, and partly as a way of addressing anxieties about immigrants from the former French colonies into France.[32] One of the participants in Kaiser's and Groult's 1977 press conference on the issue, for example, was New Right philosopher Alain de Benoist, who opposed immigration and argued against the feasibility of assimilation.[33] These positions are by no means identical with those of Kaiser; that is not my argument. But a politics of anti-politics simply left issues such as these by definition unresolved and open to appropriation by both left- and right-wing politics.

II. Cheryl Benard, Edit Schlaffer, and *Amnesty for Women*

In 1981, not long after Rupert Neudeck and others founded *Cap Anamur*, two Austrian sociologists, Cheryl Benard (b. 1953) and Edit Schlaffer (b. 1950), announced a feminist human rights organization aimed at the Third World, especially Muslim countries and among those, especially Afghanistan. They gave it the English name *Amnesty for Women*. With a manifesto in the prestigious West German newsweekly *Die Zeit* and a lecture tour, they recruited donations and members; they also soon published a book on their efforts to aid Afghan women in Pakistan's refugee camps.[34] Benard had a background in Middle Eastern studies. She researched her dissertation on Arab nationalism at the American University of Beirut and took her doctoral degree from the University of Vienna. She and Schlaffer, who likewise held a doctorate in sociology, wrote on feminist issues in Austria and Europe as well, including a pioneering book on domestic violence and marital rape in 1978.[35] They were obviously serious feminists; they may have also once been *tiersmondistes*, but now they certainly were not. They fused feminism, human rights, and postcolonial humanitarianism into an impassioned and even pugnacious justification for intervention in Third World countries.

Their writings in the early 1980s were similar in content and tone to such key texts of 1970s French *anti-tiersmondisme* as Pascal Bruckner's *The Tears of the White Man*. Like Bruckner, they combined outrage with sarcasm, and like Bruckner they criticized fellow Europeans at least as much as oppressive leaders in the Third World. Their tone was very different from Edmond Kaiser's dreamy radicalism: in their book, they opened a chapter on Muslim (actually Afghan) practices with the sarcastic disclaimer, "You thought this book was an earnest attempt to illuminate other cultures in a sympathetic and value-free manner? Then we have to excuse ourselves for the misunderstanding. Our position: sick is sick."[36] In their 1981 manifesto, reprinted in the book, they expressed their indignation that Third World national liberation revolutionaries could have demanded their own freedom from "perfidious imperialists," only to become abusers in their own right:

> Then they stand up, these breathlessly testifying revolutionaries from the colonies, and summon up their culture and traditions in order to liquidate minorities, torture opponents, arrange mass executions. To ensure that half of their people live their lives in darkness and isolation, bereft of opportunity and in humiliation.
> Let's say a sad farewell to the romanticism of revolution. Goodbye, Third World.[37]

Benard and Schlaffer positioned themselves as marginal voices confronting multiple reluctant or even hostile audiences. These were, in their interpretation, other European feminists (whose own vocabulary of oppression was, they said, totally inadequate to Third World women's sufferings), European men (who thought feminists were man-haters), Third World solidarity activists (who excused all flaws in the newly independent states by referring to colonialism), male humanitarians (who loved to dress up in turbans in the Pakistani camps and claimed it was too hard to help the sequestered women there),[38] Third World men (who ruthlessly exploited women), and Third World women (who seemed not to object to their own suffering). What was going on now was far worse than colonialism: "the Third World, speaking in general and with a few exceptions, is a place of oppression for women that makes any imperialist exploitation appear clumsy and kindhearted."[39] Pieties about sovereignty and self-determination for Third World nation-states had to be cast aside; what was needed was uncompromising intervention in the name of human rights, specifically women's human rights.

Benard and Schlaffer agreed with the Third World solidarity movement's analysis of disparities between the First and Third Worlds. They then immediately set those disparities aside to focus on what they saw as the main point: Third World men's refusal to practice solidarity with Third World women, which in turn infuriated them as European women:

> One can feel fury, even hate, for those who have so much more power and knowledge and education and opportunities and respect. For men, that is, who have *so* many advantages and are so little generous. Men who could love their daughters and their wives, but are prepared to repudiate them in the name of a masculine superiority.[40]

Benard and Schlaffer compared Third World women to political prisoners of Third World men, hence the name *Amnesty for Women*.[41]

> One is tempted to write sentences that compare women's fate in these countries to that of political prisoners and prisoners of war; of pariahs; of slaves. They must bow their heads and cover them; they must conceal themselves; they are not permitted to see the world, or if at all then only through the latticework of an absurd veiling; they are not permitted to study, to read, or to know anything, to say anything; they are to be silent and submissive and of course chaste, that is especially important.[42]

The male postcolonial leadership of the Third World was the real culprit, they argued. Frustrated with both European and Afghan men's refusal to help Afghan women in the camps, Benard and Schlaffer reported, they even found themselves thinking, why not let the Soviets stay and "re-educate" all the Afghan men![43] In their 1981 manifesto, they expanded their experiences in those camps to all of the Muslim world, if not Third World:

> What is at stake here? It is very simple, if we don't allow ourselves to be blinded by the myths and fantasies of masculine revolution. It is about human rights, about the fact, not really all that controversial, that girls should also live and should spend their lives, to the extent possible, halfway pleasantly. Not in the dark back courtyard of a clay house, while the fine gentlemen (and compared to his sister almost every male is a fine gentleman) sun themselves on the terrace. Not behind a black fabric grille, while the fine gentlemen sing revolutionary songs in the streets of Kabul, Peshawar, and Tehran with their shirts unbuttoned down to their navels. [...] A revolutionary call for the human rights of women is not to be expected from these men. Nor from their governments, unless one happens to catch a gentleman magnate from the Gulf in a calm moment in the Omar Khayyam Club in London and wins him over temporarily to the emancipation of women, women whom he has been careful to leave behind in Dubai.[44]

Only European women brave enough to confront the myths are willing to intervene, and human rights is their supposedly post-ideological justification:

> The revolutionary zeal of women in the Third World is slight. Is the West a know-it-all all over again, when it poses the question of their treatment? Is it neocolonialism, ethnocentrism, disrespect for cultural values, when one intervenes in the family affairs of other countries? If we want to answer this question with 'yes,' then we must give up the belief in human rights and halt any dialogue about justice and change. Then we will not get beyond paying homage to the superstitions of our time.[45]

Like Bruckner and other anti-totalitarian *anti-tiersmondistes* in France, Benard and Schlaffer clothed their important points in over-simplication. Moreover, to some extent they were pushing at an open door. The deprivations of Afghan women have indeed proved durable, but Benard and Schlaffer were not as isolated as they suggest in perceiving those deprivations. They do speak more elsewhere in their writings of solidarity with Afghan women, rather than assuming the latter's passivity and speaking for them.[46] Their 1981 manifesto does read like an updated version of nineteenth-century imperial feminism, yet as Anne McClintock has noted, the situation to which Benard and Schlaffer sought to draw attention has its own specificities.[47]

Benard and Schlaffer have gone on to successful and prolific careers as authors and consultants, with particular expertise on women in Muslim countries. Between 1978 and today, they have co-authored some thirty books on feminism, youth, marriage, and families, with settings of Europe, the Middle East, and Afghanistan. Benard, alone and together with Schlaffer, has written on honor violence, female genital cutting, female infanticide and, forced veiling, as well as writing novels.[48] In recent years Benard has worked in the United States as an analyst for the RAND Corporation, specializing in women and youth in the Middle East and Afghanistan, in which capacity she has publicized her concept of the "moderate Muslim."[49] Her career as a humanitarian activist and policy expert as well as her longstanding marriage to Afghan-born Zalmay Khalilzad (ambassador to Afghanistan, Iraq, and the United Nations under George W. Bush's administration) have offered her opportunities for influence on US policy.[50] From the early 1980s to today, her vision of action in the Third World is feminist nation-building in order to overcome what she sees as rigid tradition.

III. Rupert Neudeck and *Cap Anamur*

At the time of the 'boat people' crisis, Rupert Neudeck (b. 1939) was a journalist at the Cologne radio station known for its serious political reporting, *Deutschlandfunk*.[51] He met Glucksmann in early 1979 while in Paris to interview Sartre.[52] He had long been deeply concerned with ethical public action. As a young adult, he at first studied for the priesthood and entered the Jesuit order. He then left the order, married, and wrote a doctoral dissertation in philosophy on political ethics in the work of Albert Camus and Jean-Paul Sartre.[53] Soon thereafter, in 1977, he joined *Deutschlandfunk*. His humanitarian work that began in 1979 is almost as old, then, as his journalistic career.

Like so many in West Germany at that time, Neudeck had his own experience of suffering connected to war and violence. As a six-year-old at the end of the Second World War, he fled with his mother and siblings from Danzig (today Gdańsk, Poland), and barely missed embarking on the *Wilhelm Gustloff*, a ship sunk by the Soviets in one of the biggest civilian maritime disasters ever. That near-miss, he said, made the predicament of the 'boat people' vivid to him. Neudeck has compared his and other Germans' postwar refugee experience to that of refugees around the world whom he has sought to aid.[54] He has also invoked the Nazi-era past as a reason for Germans to show bravery against oppression. "My worst inheritance, against which I always had to struggle, was our cowardice. Cowardice before the Nazis and an unconscionable machinery of mass murder. I wish never to be cowardly again. Cap Anamur is the best result of the German demand *never again to be cowardly*, but rather *courageous*!"[55] Such comments highlight how humanitarian work could stem not only from a turning outward to reach other people, but also from one's own preoccupations or the preoccupations of one's own society. Here, the West German imperative of "never again" war, fascism, and genocide clearly shaped his humanitarian work.

Neudeck specifically distanced courageous, moral action from the state. He recalled asking Sartre, back in 1979, what young people ought to do, and cited with full approval Sartre's answer:

> 'We are all alienated from institutions, alienated from the state, alienated from people, who are in turn alienated from themselves. One must seek to break these relationships of alienation. One must try to live for oneself and for others. One must realize oneself by giving oneself to others!'

Neudeck recalled, "To me that sounded just like the gospel." Then Sartre linked helping others to the very public task of preserving democracy: "One must try to act on behalf of those who are at present the most threatened and marginalized, one must make a permanent effort so that true democracy may exist." Yet Sartre ruled out any meaningful role for the state here. As Neudeck recalled,

> He rejected the state with a rigor that I recognized and learned to value only much later. [Sartre said] 'We must rediscover a worthwhile [*wertvolle*] society in which one can live for others and for oneself. But one cannot reach this worthwhile, human society through institutions, but rather only through action, in the actions of each and every person. Through moral action, that is, for action for the sake of others is always a moral deed.'[56]

Neudeck here shows his connections to the French 'antitotalitarian moment' of the 1970s, when as historian Michael Scott Christofferson shows, figures on the non-Communist Left sought to reinvent democracy through various forms of spontaneity and decentering of authority.[57]

All four of the humanitarians briefly discussed here have distanced themselves from ideology and have emphasized their own freedom to move through this world, make unmediated contact with others, and radically change lives. They claim, as the justification for their actions, the immediate experience of suffering. This supposedly apolitical motivation to act in response to suffering, without or even against states, was clearly central to the new subjectivity these and other 1970s humanitarians were developing.[58] It is not surprising that they highlight their own agency, since they are seeking to persuade those who have not seen the suffering firsthand, and who may doubt the feasibility of the humanitarian's project. At the same time, these humanitarians' references to immediate sympathy serve to disqualify political discussion, even as the effects of their work are manifestly political. All four of them proudly display their disrespect for state sovereignty, in the very decades of its greatest proliferation. Kaiser and Neudeck moreover emphasize their supposed race-blindness. They thereby bolster their own legitimacy over both the colonialism of the past and the regimes of the present that were founded on anticolonial nationalism. Benard and Schlaffer, by contrast, do not make claims for the possibility of non-Europeans' seamless integration into Europe, and they make the strongest arguments about what they see as persistent unenlightened, uncivilized tradition.

What specific form of postcoloniality do they inhabit? One can easily point to what seem like powerful continuities between the humanitarianism of the last several decades and the era of formal colonialism. There are at least two problems with doing so, however. First, the era of formal colonialism may thereby appear in an oversimplified light, as if it were one coherent project. Second, the new subjectivities of these humanitarian actors, best displayed through their own writings, may be overlooked. These humanitarians consciously act in a context where colonialism has lost legitimacy, and also a context in which the Holocaust and mass death under state socialism have been received as facts requiring a new (anti-)politics. What is new, therefore, should not be mistaken for the old. Their strident claims to being agents, to being in the right, and to navigate freely between the First and Third Worlds may be reminiscent of colonial attitudes, but may also be fruitful for a more challenging project of picking apart assumptions of what being post- as well as anti-colonial need entail.

Notes:

[1] The epigraph here came from a public lecture: Rupert Neudeck, "Die tödliche Macht der Naturkatastrophen," 10 Feb. 2009, hosted by Albertus-Magnus-Forum, Cologne, Germany. It is a paraphrase based on my notes. On 28 June 2009 *Cap Anamur* held an anniversary event and its website contains texts of the presentations there. See Rupert Neudeck, "On revient toujours a ses premieres amours. Rede beim 30jährigen Jubiläums-Fest der Cap Anamur in der Kölner Trinitatis Kirche," www.capanamur.org/pressemitteilungen (accessed 21 Oct. 2012). Unless otherwise noted, all translations from German and French are my own.

[2] Neudeck, "On revient," 1. See similar passages about "the deed" and about how *Cap Anamur* was not founded, but rather "emerged spontaneously" in Rupert Neudeck, Abenteuer Menschlichkeit. Erinnerungen (Cologne: Kiepenheuer & Witsch, 2007), 55, 85.

[3] See www.medecinsdumonde.org, then choose "Médecins du Monde," then "Histoire et valeurs," then "Historique" (accessed 21 Oct. 2012).

[4] "Dr. Rupert Neudeck, Cap Anamur, im Gespräch mit Wolfgang Küpper," 23 July 2002, http://www.br.de/fernsehen/br-alpha/sendungen/alpha-forum/rupert-neudeck-gespraech100.html (accessed 21 Oct. 2012).

[5] From 1979 to today, he pointed out, *Cap Anamur* had refused "the temptations of the flesh-pots of the government," i.e. state funding (Neudeck, "On revient," 1). The most that Neudeck could say for the West German government was that he and others could launch *A Ship for Vietnam* because "we lived in a free society," that is, he and others were able to act, not because their state

helped them, but because it left them alone. The West German state did eventually obstruct them more seriously, however: in 1982 *Cap Anamur* had to stop the rescues of 'boat people,' because the Federal Republic refused to admit any more of those refugees.

[6] Neudeck, "On revient," 4. The passage is from Albert Camus, The Plague, trans. Stuart Gilbert (New York: Vintage, 1991), 210. See also Neudeck's discussion of Camus's influence on him in Neudeck, Abenteuer Menschlichkeit, 241-5.

[7] Neudeck, "Die tödliche Macht." Neudeck was probably referring to UN Resolution 43/131 of 8 December 1988 and associated resolutions. See Bernard Kouchner, Le Malheur des Autres (Paris: Editions Odile Jacobs, 1991), 331-3.

[8] See the "Medienecho" section of the *Cap Anamur* website, www.cap-anamur.org, and choose the year 2009 for a summary of the case (accessed 21 Oct. 2012).

[9] Michael Barnett and Thomas G. Weiss, Humanitarianism in Question. Politics, Power, Ethics (Ithaca: Cornell University Press, 2008); David Rieff, A Bed for the Night. Humanitarianism in Crisis (New York: Simon and Schuster, 2002); Richard A. Wilson and Richard D. Brown, Humanitarianism and Suffering. The Mobilization of Empathy (New York: Cambridge University Press, 2009). On German-speaking humanitarians, see Nina Berman, Impossible Missions? German Economic, Military, and Humanitarian Efforts in Africa (Lincoln, NE: University of Nebraska Press, 2004).

[10] See Michael Scott Christofferson, French Intellectuals Against the Left. The Anti-Totalitarian Moment of the 1970s (New York: Berghahn, 2003).

[11] Partha Chatterjee, The Nation and Its Fragments. Colonial and Postcolonial Histories (Princeton: Princeton University Press, 1993), 16-8.

[12] See Paul Kennedy, The Parliament of Man. The Past, Present, and Future of the United Nations (New York: Vintage, 2006).

[13] On these new techniques, see Kenneth Cmiel, "The Emergence of Human Rights Politics in the United States," Journal of American History 86,3 (1999): 1231-50. On the term "postcolonial," see Anne McClintock, "The Angel of Progress. Pitfalls of the Term 'Post-Colonialism'," Social Text 31-32 (1992): 84-92.

[14] See Kristin Ross, May '68 and Its Afterlives (Chicago: University of Chicago Press, 2002), 158-69. She discusses Samir Amin et al., eds., Le tiers monde et la gauche (Paris: Seuil, 1979) and Pascal Bruckner, The Tears of the White Man. Compassion as Contempt, trans. and with an introduction by William R. Beer (New York: Free Press, 1986), originally published in French in 1983. For vital French political context, see Christofferson, French Intellectuals Against the Left. See also Bernard Taithe, "Reinventing (French) Universalism. Religion, Humanitarianism and the 'French Doctors'," Modern and Contemporary France 12 (2004): 147-58.

[15] See Neudeck, Abenteuer Menschlichkeit, 66-70 (Glucksmann), 234-40

(Sartre) and Rupert Neudeck, Die Menschenretter von Cap Anamur (Munich: C. H. Beck, 2002), 24-6 (Sartre), 26 (Kouchner).

[16] This biographical information is drawn from Christophe Gallaz, Entretiens avec Edmond Kaiser. Fondateur de Terre des Hommes. Cofondateur de Sentinelles (Lausanne: Editions Favre, 1998); Kaiser's obituary in the New York Times, 8 Mar. 2000; Edmond Kaiser, La Marche aux enfants (Lausanne: P.-M. Favre, 1979). The fictionalized account of his son's death is: Edmond Kaiser, Mémorial d'une poupée (Lausanne: Editions de l'Aire, 1985).

[17] *Terre des Hommes* was named after St. Exupéry's 1939 memoir Terre des Hommes, which was translated as Wind, Sand and Stars, trans. Lewis Galantière (New York: Reynal & Hitchcock, 1939). The name *Sentinelles* was drawn from a passage in that book about the importance of taking care of other people. See St. Exupéry, Wind, Sand and Stars, 295 or St. Exupéry, Oeuvres complètes, Vol. I (Paris: Gallimard, 1994), 280.

[18] Gallaz, Entretiens, 7.

[19] A revisionist study of Camus useful in this context of humanitarianism is: David Carroll, Albert Camus the Algerian. Colonialism, Terrorism, Justice (New York: Columbia University Press, 2007).

[20] Terre des Femmes, ed., Tod als Ehrensache. Frauenschicksale (Berlin: Verlag für Wissenschaft und Bildung, 1989), 20. This book is a translation of Sentinelles, ed., Princesses mortes (Lausanne: Sentinelles, 1981).

[21] "Avant-propos," in Les mutilations sexuelles féminines. Mariage précoce, ed. Sentinelles (Lausanne: Sentinelles, 1980), 4. The French version is on 3, and I have used it to improve the English version here.

[22] Gallaz, Entretiens, 57-8.

[23] Ibid., 35-9, 43.

[24] Ibid., 33. See the website of that organization in its current form, www.emmaus-international.org (accessed 21 Oct. 2012).

[25] Kaiser, La Marche aux enfants, 262.

[26] I have not been able to discover how honor violence first came to his attention. He learned of the practice of female genital cutting when he read French feminist Benoïte Groult's 1975 manifesto Ainsi soit-elle (Editions Grassel & Fasquelle, 1975). See "Talkrunde," in Leben heißt frei sein. Internationaler Kongress für Frauen- und Menschenrechte. 12.-13. Oktober 2001, Berlin. Dokumentation, ed. Terre des Femmes (Tübingen: Terre des Femmes, 2002), 161. He held a press conference with Groult in 1977 to publicize the issue and pressure the WHO and UN. See the record of that press conference: Terre des Hommes, ed., Les mutilations sexuelles féminines infligée aux enfants (Geneva: Terre des Hommes, 1977). The media covered it broadly; see e.g. "Sache des Bluts," Der Spiegel, 6 June 1977.

[27] Gallaz, Entretiens, 38. Kaiser founded yet other initiatives and organizations over his long life, and one of them, La petite Espérance (1990) made exclusion

from other criteria its main criterion. It was aimed at "girls and women or other sufferers who fall outside the 'criteria' of ordinary organizations." Ibid., 145.

[28] Its publications include Sentinelles, ed., Les mutilations and Sentinelles, ed., Princesses mortes (Lausanne: Sentinelles, 1981). See also the website www.sentinelles.org (accessed 21 Oct. 2012).

[29] Gallaz, Entretiens, 58-9.

[30] On "interracial adoption," a phrase to which Kaiser objected, and Amadou's life in Lausanne, see Kaiser, La Marche, 263, 269-71. On nationalist and Muslim barriers to adoption, see ibid., 244, 269.

[31] E.g. Neudeck, Abenteuer Menschlichkeit, 82-4 and Neudeck, "Die tödliche Macht der Naturkatastrophen."

[32] See Eloïse A. Brière, "Confronting the Western Gaze," in Female Circumcision and the Politics of Knowledge. African Women in Imperialist Discourse, ed. Obioma Nnaemeka (Westport: Praeger, 2005), 165-80, and Bronwyn Winter, "Women, the Law, and Cultural Relativism in France. The Case of Excision," Signs 19,4 (1994): 939-74.

[33] Alain de Benoist, "Les mutilations sexuelles. Clitoridectomie, infibulation," in Les mutilations, ed. Terre des Hommes, 25-8.

[34] Cheryl Benard and Edit Schlaffer, "Sie müssen ihr Haupt beugen. Ein Plädoyer für die Menschenrechte," Die Zeit, 30 Oct. 1981. It was republished in their book Die Grenzen des Geschlechts. Anleitungen zum Sturz des Internationalen Patriarchats. Amnesty for Women (Reinbek bei Hamburg: Rowohlt, 1984), 9-12.

[35] Cheryl Benard and Edit Schlaffer, Die ganz gewöhnliche Gewalt in der Ehe. Texte zu einer Soziologie von Macht und Liebe (Reinbek bei Hamburg: Rowohlt, 1978).

[36] Benard and Schlaffer, Die Grenzen, 125.

[37] Benard and Schlaffer, "Sie müssen ihr Haupt beugen."

[38] Benard and Schlaffer, Die Grenzen, 272, 278-9. They were too early to overlap with Rupert Neudeck and others from *Cap Anamur*, but the latter may have fit this image: in 1987, *Cap Anamur* started an ill-fated mission that is not always included in its official histories. With the intention of opening a hospital in a region the mujaheddin had retaken from the Soviets, some *Cap Anamur* workers entered from Peshawar, Pakistan. The groups came under Soviet fire and had to flee. See "Vagabund im Dienst der Humanität. Werner Höfner engagiert sich seit 1982 für Cap Anamur – oft unter Lebensgefahr," Süddeutsche Zeitung, 24 Mar. 2009 and Rupert Neudeck, Jenseits von Kabul. Unterwegs in Afghanistan (Munich: C. H. Beck, 2003). In more recent years, since the US invasion, *Cap Anamur* is building village schools for girls there.

[39] Benard and Schlaffer, "Sie müssen ihr Haupt beugen."

[40] Eaed.

[41] They explicitly described their new organization as applying the *Amnesty International* model to women. See eaed. At the time *Amnesty International*

was the object of wider criticism for its refusal to take women's human rights on board.

[42] Eaed.

[43] Benard and Schlaffer, Die Grenzen, 275.

[44] Benard and Schlaffer, "Sie müssen ihr Haupt beugen."

[45] Eaed.

[46] This is true to a limited extent in the 1984 book, but much more true of more recent publications, such as a book on the Revolutionary Association of the Women of Afghanistan (RAWA): Cheryl Benard, Veiled Courage. Inside the Afghan Women's Resistance, with the assistance of Edit Schlaffer (New York: Broadway, 2002).

[47] On imperial feminism, see Antoinette Burton, Burdens of History. British Feminists, Indian Women, and Imperial Culture 1865-1915 (Chapel Hill: University of North Carolina Press, 1994). On the need for a concept of gender power specific to many post-independence states' disenfranchisement of women, see McClintock, "Pitfalls," 92.

[48] One of her novels is set in Pakistan and Afghanistan: Benard, Moghul Buffet (New York: Farrar, Straus, Giroux, 1998). From 1982 until 2005 Benard and Schlaffer led a research institute in Vienna, the Ludwig-Boltzmann-Forschungsstelle für Politik und zwischenmenschliche Beziehungen, which focused on gender and youth topics (such as educational differences between girls and boys). In 2002 Schlaffer became director of a new organization, *Frauen ohne Grenzen* (Women Without Borders), which promotes communication between Western and Arab women and women's political leadership. See www.frauen-ohne-grenzen.org (accessed 21 Oct. 2012).

[49] Among her RAND publications, see Cheryl Benard, Civil Democratic Islam. Partners, Resources, and Strategies (Santa Monica: RAND, 2003) and Cheryl Benard, Seth G. Jones, Olga Oliker, Cathryn Quantic Thurston, Brooke Stearns Lawson, and Kristen Cordell, Women and Nation Building (Santa Monica: RAND, 2008).

[50] On Khalilzad, see Jon Lee Anderson, "American Viceroy," New Yorker, 19 Dec. 2005. Benard and Khalilzad met as students at the American University of Beirut in the 1970s.

[51] On *Deutschlandfunk*, see Neudeck, Abenteuer Menschlichkeit, 177-8.

[52] Neudeck, Abenteuer Menschlichkeit, 66-8.

[53] Ibid., 35-8. Rupert Neudeck, Die politische Ethik bei Jean-Paul Sartre und Albert Camus (Bonn: Bouvier, 1975).

[54] Neudeck, Die Menschenretter, 10-1 and Neudeck, Abenteuer Menschlichkeit, 11-7.

[55] Neudeck, "On revient," 7.

[56] Neudeck, Die Menschenretter, 26.

[57] Christofferson, French Intellectuals.

[58] An important contribution to this issue is: Michal Givoni, "Humanitarian Governance and Ethical Cultivation. Médecins Sans Frontières and the Advent of the Expert-Witness," Millennium. Journal of International Studies 40,1 (2011): 43-63. Also important here is Christofferson, French Intellectuals.

Contributors

Eva Bischoff is Assistant Professor at the Department of International History at the University of Trier. Her general research interests include the history of British, German, and US colonialism, postcolonial studies, and gender/queer studies. In 2011, she published *Kannibale-Werden. Eine postkoloniale Geschichte deutscher Männlichkeit um 1900*. Her current research project focuses on the interaction between the Religious Society of Friends (Quakers) and indigenous societies in the process of settler imperialism in the United States and Australia between 1780s and 1860s.

Manuela Bojadžijev is Assistant Professor at the Institute for European Ethnology at the Humboldt University of Berlin. Before, she has been working as a Lecturer at the Department of Sociology at Goldsmiths University of London and as a Visiting Lecturer at the New York University branch in Berlin and at City University in London. Bojadžijev co-edited the book *Konjunkturen des Rassismus* (2001), and *Turbulente Ränder. Neue Perspektiven auf Migration an den Grenzen Europas* (2007). Her single-authored book *Die windige Internationale. Rassismus und Kämpfe der Migration* was published in 2008.

Robert Júlio Decker studied Anglo-American History, Medieval and Modern History, and Political Sciences at the University of Cologne. He received his PhD from the University of Leeds for an analysis of the history of the *Immigration Restriction League* (IRL). In his project, he investigated the IRL as a nodal point of the discourses of scientific racism, eugenics, and the so-called new immigration. More generally, he works on the history of racial thought, whiteness, transnational migration policies and the progressive era.

Elisabeth Engel received her M.A. from the University of Cologne in 2008 and started teaching Postcolonial Studies and African American history at the Department of Anglo American History, University of Cologne, where she also was involved in organizing the *Brown Bag Lecture Series: Colonialism and Beyond*. In October 2009, she was awarded a doctoral fellowship by the German Research Foundation (DFG) and entered the Graduate School of North American Studies of the John F. Kennedy Institute, Free University Berlin. Her research focuses on African American missionaries in colonial Africa during the interwar years. She was a visiting PhD student at Columbia University, New York in 2012.

Serhat Karakayali is Assistant Professor at the Institute of Sociology at the University of Halle. Before his undergraduate studies in sociology at the University of Frankfurt am Main, he worked at the *Duisburger Institut für Sprach- und Sozialforschung* (DISS). He completed his dissertation on the history of illegal immigration in Germany as a scholar of the Heinrich-Böll Foundation.

Since 2003, he is one of the founding members of the research group "Transit Migration," which has been recently turned into the "Research Network Critical Migration Studies." Together with Marion von Osten und Tom Avermaete, he ran the research and exhibition project "In the Desert of Modernity."

Judith Schachter is Professor of Anthropology and History, Department of History, Carnegie Mellon University, Pittsburgh, Pennsylvania. She has been doing fieldwork in Hawai`i for over two decades, and has recently completed a manuscript on the impact of United States colonialism on the lives of individuals who identify as Native Hawaiian (forthcoming). Her published work includes articles on family and housing policies, and currently on the movement for indigenous rights in Hawai`i (forthcoming in *Social Identities*). In addition, she has published two books on adoption (*Kinship with Strangers* 1994; *A Sealed and Secret Kinship* 2002), a study of a steel town outside of Pittsburgh (*A Town Without Steel* 1998), and a biography of Ruth Fulton Benedict (1983) as well as numerous articles.

Olaf Stieglitz is a historian of twentieth-century US history. He has just finished the manuscript of his second research-based book entitled *Confidential Sources. A Cultural History of Informers & Informants in the Twentieth Century United States*. Among his research interests are gender history, the history of the body, and aspects of political culture revolving around questions of loyalty and betrayal. Stieglitz has also published on sports history as a history of modern bodies; recently he published the article "Sport und Männlichkeit" in volume edited by the Deutsches Hygiene-Museum Dresden (*Auf die Plätze. Sport und Gesellschaft*, 2011).

Lora Wildenthal is Associate Professor of History and Department Chair at Rice University in Houston, Texas, USA. She is the author of *German Women for Empire, 1884-1945* (2001), and *The Language of Human Rights in West Germany* (2012).